Ray Kampf

The Bear Handbook

A Comprehensive Guide for Those Who Are Husky, Hairy, and Homosexual and Those Who Love 'Em

Pre-publication
REVIEW

"**R**ay Kampf has put together a marvelous compilation of Bear 101 information in *The Bear Handbook*—a cross between the Boy Scout's Manual of basic survival information for any newcomer to bear culture and a cheeky camp send-up of ursine foibles and sacred cows. (What you don't eat, you can accessorize.) *The Bear Handbook* does for bears what Clark Henley's *Butch Manual* did for clone culture a couple generations ago. The pithily drawn observations (obviously 'meant in a kind and loving way,' to paraphrase Dame Edna Everage) and compilation of factual information and resources are bountifully illustrated with Kampf's artwork, which alone makes the book worth possessing. This book belongs in every bear's library, and is especially recommended for anyone who prefers to frequent restaurants that use pictures on their menus."

Les Wright, PhD
Author of *The Bear Book*
and *The Bear Book II*

The Bear Handbook

*A Comprehensive Guide for Those
Who Are Husky, Hairy, and Homosexual
and Those Who Love 'Em*

The Bear Handbook

*A Comprehensive Guide for Those
Who Are Husky, Hairy, and Homosexual
and Those Who Love 'Em*

Ray Kampf

Harrington Park Press ®
An Imprint of The Haworth Press, Inc.
New York · London · Oxford

Published by

Harrington Park Press®, an imprint of The Haworth Press, Inc.
10 Alice Street, Binghamton, NY 13904-1580

Cover design by Ray Kampf.

The Bear Flag, copyright 1995 Craig Byrnes/Bear Manufacturing. Used with
permission.

Depiction or mention of any person in this work should not be construed as an
implication of said person's sexual orientation.

Library of Congress Cataloging-in-Publication Data

The bear handbook : a comprehensive guide for those who are husky, hairy,
and homosexual, and those who love 'em / compiled by Ray Kampf.
     p. cm.
Includes bibliographical references and index.
ISBN 1-56023-996-4 (hard : alk. paper) – ISBN 1-56023-997-2 (soft : alk. paper)
1. Gay men. 2. Homosexuality, Male. 3. Gay men–Humor. 4. Gay men–Social
life and customs–20th century. I. Kampf, Ray.

HQ76 .B373 2000
305.38'9664–dc21

00-039698

The Table of Contents

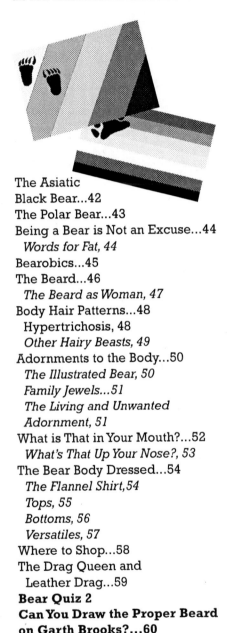

CHAPTER THREE
THE BEAR'S HABITAT

CHAPTER FOUR
WHEN A BEAR
NEEDS A BEAR

CHAPTER FIVE
THE LEFTOVERS

ABOUT THE AUTHOR

Ray Kampf has been studying the species of Bear men for close to a decade. He has done field work traveling to the ends of the earth in search of this rare breed. From grizzlies to cubs, Ray has closely examined Bears, spending hours in their watering holes and partaking in their ritual social habits. He has attended events and made scientific observations to chronicle the mating rituals and sexual encounters of the male Bear in the wild and in captivity. He himself is a Bear and as such was able to blend into the society of big hairy men to put down on paper that which only has been discussed over Bud Lights and over the Internet.

Ray, who happily cohabitates with his own husbear Jim, holds a BFA in Communication Design from Kutztown University, home of the Golden Bears.

Foreword

Les Wright

The Bear Handbook does for Beardom what *The Butch Manual* did for gay clones. It is the most up-to-date, informative summary of Bear culture disguised as a parody. Ray Kampf walks a wickedly fine line between the truth and lies which tell a higher truth.

Bear culture emerged rapidly and proliferated around planet Earth before most folks knew what hit them. For the uninitiated this is a crash course in everything Bearish; for the insider it's a firm rap on the knuckles for getting too full of oneself. The factual information is profusely illustrated, but the real heart and soul of Ray's tongue-in-cheek how-to and who's who manual is the way in which it captures the original Bear spirit. Before there were sash queens (or rather, sash Bears), Bear contests were in fact a form of Bear camp, of making fun of those in the queer community who take themselves all too seriously, as well as shattering the barrier, which humor does so well, allowing Bears to tell jokes on ourselves as gay men who had previously felt excluded by the larger gay community.

This book has validated me in my practice of transforming great works of art into Bear jack-off images. It conjured fond memories of a young Sean Connery, who as Zardoz ran around the year 2292 in little more than a buckskin bikini. I even raised an eyebrow at the inclusion of Cliff, the IHOP guy, as a model bear. (He's the guy who goes around asking everyone— little girls, little boys, farmers, truck drivers— to join him "for breakfast" at any time of the day or night.) Most Bears have better taste, if not better manners.

Asking "what is a Bear?" is akin to asking "why is the sky blue?" One is not asking so much for an answer as for a smack in the chops for being a smart-ass. Nonetheless, Ray answers this question by exemplifying many of Beardom's contradictory manifestations, poking fun at himself and at us Bears as a whole. PC flies out the window, and Bear PC most of all. And Ray captures another essence of gay Bears— in our social roles as healers, tricksters, and large subversive imps— as real men masquerading as real men.

ACKNOWLEDGMENTS

Bill Palmer, The Tragic Tuesday Gang, Bobby (Bobby, Baby, Bobby, Bubby) Singer, LTV, The BML, The B.O.C.F., Kevin and Johnny, Les Wright, Cover Man 56, Marylouise, Trish Brown, Karen Fisher, Forrest, Photoshop Shelly, Keith and Matt who I should have known about in college, MVP soon to be Mrs. MVP, Lynn Ludwig, Lurch, Josh, Karen Carpenter, Bear Manufacturing, Mikey, Steve Perry, David and Jason of the LA David and Jasons, The Haworth Press, The Seattle Pharmacist, Ed the Once Bartender, The Full Moon Saloon, The Denver Gold Medalist, The Owner of the Used "A" Frame Camper, Peaches, Lil' John, The Cuban and the Guatamalan and their partners, The Team Coach, The Jeweler/Flattopper, Brad, The Stealth Mushroomer, The Web, The M.D. Down Under, John from Pittsburgh, Jimmy, Wade, The Leprechaun from San Diego, Anyone I've ever met on ICUII, AOL, ICQ, or IRC, the Franklin Minter, all the Bears that answered a survey, The Orlando Santa, That Military Bear Across the Pond, Lisa Birnbach, The Late Great Joey the Klepto, The Exterminating Slut, Sharon McColon, The Ventura Bears, The Queen Mum, Ogie, Mr. Weekly, Fireplug and Larry, Doug the Aerobics Instructor, The Tonsil Hockey Team at IBR 98, The Twinks from Philly, Jill and Robbie, who know how to bike, Matt the Fringe Guy and City Boy Ben—both straight but not narrow, BrianMD@brianmd.com,

And of course, Jim

Introduction

As with a lot of good things, this started in a bar. It was early in the summer and the local news being broadcast on the bar TV was heralding the debut of Dolly, the cloned sheep of England. My other half quipped that cloning is nothing new. "Just look around the bar." He was right. I would be hard pressed to meet a blind date here if the visual description I had was "stocky build, bearded and wearing a flannel shirt." Like the Castro Clones of two decades earlier, the Bear men now find themselves trying to fit a certain look and act a certain way. They are trying to become a certain stereotype.

I have always had a love-hate relationship with stereotypes. I know that every Italian is not greasy, that every Polack is not dumb and that every queer is not Liberace, thank God. But let's face it, without stereotypes, some jokes just wouldn't be funny. Some aspects of humor rely on stereotypical generalizations. A smart person with an open mind knows this. Intelligence and humor go hand in hand. And a minority joke is always funnier when a member of the minority presents it. Joan Rivers tells a mean JAP joke. Tim Allen has been known to tell a good man-bashing joke now and then. And although I have never heard a battered woman tell a wife-abuse joke, it has the potential to be a real knee slapper. With this philosophy, my lover and I decided that there needed to be a Bear Handbook that made broad generalizations and outlined all the aspects of stereotypical Bear life. So that my fellow hairy big guys wouldn't show up at the bar in biker shorts or rent the wrong porn tape, we talked to a lot of Bear men, pored over issues of *Bear* magazine, made trips to Bear events and surfed the web — an arduous task but we felt obligated. We made assumptions about the Bear stereotypes and when researched, found that, oddly enough, like any stereotype, they had a basis of truth.

One truth we found is that Bears have a good sense of humor and are relatively intelligent. Bears reading this book should realize that all Bears really do not fit these or any stereotypes. The Bear community is made up of individuals just like any minority. And yes, not all Bears will fit all the criteria listed in this book. However, there are some Bears who will, and those are the ones we can laugh at.

Ray
2000

CHAPTER ONE

EMERGENCE FROM THE WOODS

*the history of the breed and
where they come from*
or
"Realizing that real men are not
in the pages of GQ"

WHAT IS A BEAR?

We all have our own definition of what a Bear is. To children, a bear is a snuggly stuffed thing you take to bed with you. To most of the world a bear is a fierce forest creature covered in hair with a definite attitude and voracious appetite. In the gay community, a Bear is that guy at the White Party making too many trips to the chips and dip. But what truly defines a Bear are three things: Size, Hair and being Gay. There are those thin hairy nambi-pambi twinks who will say, "I'm a Bear, because I think I'm a Bear." Or those in the Girth and Mirth Club who haven't a strand of hair on their chest who say, "I'm a Bear, because I have the right attitude." Well, they're wrong. A Bear has at least a size 36 waist, a goatee (it better be a full goatee; not the wisps of hair seen on a club kid) and will gladly be on his knees other than at church.

SIZE— A Bear can consume a large amount of beer and pizza. Obviously these are not fat-free. This is not to say that all Bears are fat, but Bears do have bulk. It could be muscle, it could be mass or it could be those little chocolate doughnuts. In any case a Bear looks better fuller. The size can come from genetics. Ideally, after a lifelong battle of the bulge the Bear finally accepts that Richard Simmons is the enemy and learns to love his body. Or his heftiness can come from age: Once the queen of disco with aspirations to be on MTV's "The Grind," the Bear grows out of fashions from Chess King and into his new body due largely to overconsumption at after-rave parties at IHOP.

HAIR— What was seen as a curse in junior high school has become the hallmark of a Bear: a good pelt of fur matted across the chest. Very often as an added bonus, the hair creeps up to the shoulders and on to the back. Bears have the natural ability, thanks to their mother's side of the family, to grow a full Beard in a matter of weeks, if not days. There is no such thing as 5 o'clock shadow with a Bear; there is, however, 10 a.m. shadow. The only place where hair is an option for Bears is on top of their head. While many other men go through midlife crises hoping the Hair Club for Men will save them from male pattern baldness, Bears celebrate their scalp. Sometimes by shaving even more hair off.

BEING GAY— Bears are a tactile species. They like to touch and be touched…. and not delicately. Roughhousing among real Bears in the woods is a form of social play.

Their human counterparts have adopted this play and found that being among men who aren't afraid to touch and feel is a wonderful thing. In our society, that's called being gay. Sure, there are heterosexual Bears in terms of size and hair. And those straight Bears may even like roughhousing on the football field, in a wrestling ring or a bar fight. But it is doubtful that those straight Bears want to pick out window treatments with their opponent. A Gay Bear just might.

There are those who would expand this list to include attributes such as friendliness, a flannel shirt, a good sense of humor, and knowing all the dialogue to *Steel Magnolias*. And in a way those are valid qualifications. But what it boils down to, when a Bear needs a Bear, is that he wants the right size man with the right amount of hair who is willing to do things that Jesse Helms says are wrong.

Bear, Not a Bear

Buzz, not Woody
Oscar, not Felix
Garth Brooks, not Chris Gaines
The Hulk, not Dr. Bruce Banner
Ernie, not Bert
Hardy, not Laurel
Green Arrow, not Green Lantern
Vanzetti, not Sacco
Edina, not Patsy
Jud Fry, not Curly
(movie version)
Skipper, not Gilligan
Brooks, not Dunn
Silent Bob, not Jay
Sodom, not Gomorrah
Wolfman, not Dracula
Hoss, not Little Joe
Fred Flintstone, not George Jetson
George, not Kramer
Hyde, not Jekyll
Commander Riker, not Mr. Spock
Ethel, not Lucy
Al, not Tim
R2D2, not C3PO
(of course R2D2
could be a lesbian)

Beards & Bears in History & Film

In the beginning, there was God and he had a Beard. And it was good. This is according to Michelangelo, and because nobody can say for sure how God really looks, we often think of the Sistine Chapel as a point of reference. You can see it being painted in *The Agony and the Ecstasy* starring Charlton Heston.

If you're a Darwinian, then man evolved out of the primordial soup without a razor in his hand. Caveman, the natural man, let the fur on his cheeks grow, like the beasts in the forest. This is clearly seen in *Quest for Fire*. In either case, Beards have been around for a long time and the adornment of facial hair has gone in and out of style through the ages. But best of all you can rent the history of the beard in your local video store.

The Egyptians thought beards and facial hair were lower class, so they shaved their bodies. (And they're thought of as a great civilization?) Still, both men and women donned prosthetic beards for special occasions.

Zeus, Poseidon, Gods, Beards...
...Put it together!

Many men in Rome wore beards. Except in the military, where it could be detrimental. Facial hair gave an enemy something to grab onto as he slit your throat. Still, noblemen and senators wore them, as did Emperors. Emperor Hadrian could very well be considered the first Bear: He was masculine, he was bearded and he was gay.

Members of the Elizabethan Court, such as Sir Walter Raleigh and William Shakespeare, regarded facial hair as a means of expression. The artistry of extreme styles led to the pointed Van Dyke by the time Charles I took the throne.

Norsemen had beards, but they were savagely kept.

The Explorers of the New World had beards— sailors, you know.

King Henry VIII brought beards back into fashion despite the fact that wearing a beard was taxable.

---

caveman | egyptians | **greeks** | romans | **vikings** | medieval | **tudor** | renaissance

---

The Steve Reeves Era: His chest made him a matinee idol, his tan made him a gay icon, his beard made him a Bear. He played Hercules in a number of films; most of them really bad.

Clash of the Titans

The Lion in Winter

Excalibur

Hamlet (the Mel Gibson version)

Braveheart Bears in abundance

The Age of Sean Connery: 007 doubles as a Medieval chameleon playing a range of Bears of the Middle Ages. He portrayed a monk (*Name of the Rose*), the Green Knight (*Sword of the Valiant*), an older Robin Hood (*Robin and Marian*) and kings Arthur and Richard the Lion Hearted (*First Knight* and *Robin Hood, Prince of Thieves*). One of the few men who can make armor and a monk's robe look sexy.

Beards & Robes: The Biblical Epic is born. Moses and Samson appear on the silver screen, Tony Curtis is cruised by Lawrence Olivier in *Spartacus* and Gladiator movies become the predecessor to gay porn.

The Brian Blessed Stage: Shakespeare did not write porno, but Brian brings much Bear sex appeal to the Bard's work *Henry V* and *Much Ado About Nothing* (which is a beard marathon by itself). But his work goes beyond the Renaissance. He's done toga epics (*I, Claudius* and *The Last Days of Pompeii*) and played Long John Silver (*Return to Treasure Island*). He is truly the Bear Master Thespian.

Louis XIII was put on the throne in France at a young age and had no facial hair. So beards fell out of vogue. This is the first time the French start dictating fashion. A beard was looked upon as a sign of a foreigner and someone not to be trusted. Beards took a while to come back into social circles. They were, however, popular among Swashbucklers and Cutthroats.

Ulysses S. Grant and Robert E. Lee, two full-bearded men, rose to the top of the Union and the Confederacy in a war that pitted brother against brother. It also laid the groundwork for Civil War reenactments throughout the East Coast. Uniform night at local bars looks like a James Brady photograph gone awry.

Bear U.S. Presidents
Abraham Lincoln 1861-1865
Gen. Ulysses S. Grant 1869-1877
Rutherford B. Hayes 1877-1881
James A. Garfield 1881
Chester A. Arthur 1881-1885
Benjamin Harrison 1889-1893

Teddy Roosevelt— Not bearded but a notable man in Bear History, for he is the namesake of the Teddy Bear.

The Golden Era of Beards
The Victorian era finessed and refined goatees and handlebar moustaches. Any man with any stature in society had to have facial hair of some sort. Even the presidency had a significant run of furryface commanders-in-chief.

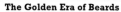

The Mountain Men start to move to Western America and Grizzly Adams is born 1812

In Bavaria, Mad King Ludwig builds a fairytale castle, falls in love with Richard Wagner and mysteriously dies. He also sports a full muzzle of facial hair.

The Hippies bring the natural look back and the beard is reborn.

restoration	19th cent.	civil war	western	victorian	turn of the century	modern

Pirates and Musketeers
There's BlackBeard, BlueBeard and YellowBeard, all pirates in movies, but the films *Pirates* by Roman Polanski and Disney's *Treasure Island* really capture the bearishness of pirate life. Tim Curry, on the other hand, played Long John Silver in *Muppet Treasure Island* as Dr. Frank N. Furter in a beard.
Meanwhile in France, Faye Dunaway and Raquel Welch were running around with the Three (and then 4 and 5) Musketeers. Remakes have been done and the rule is: Porthos is always a Bear (Oliver Platt in the 1993 version). However most of us fell for the Hanna Barbera version on the Banana Splits. He was a cartoon, but he was hot!

The early cowboy films showed mostly pretty boys in starched shirts on horseback, however *Silverado* brought Bears to the Old West. Kevin Kline, Brian Dennehy, John Cleese and Danny Glover, all a little rough around the edges and full beards on their chins.

Gettysburg

Glory

20,000 Leagues Under the Sea James Mason has the best beard in film history.

WWII was a Bear war at sea only in *Das Boot*. Americans were clean shaven.

The American Epic The War Between the States became the inspiration for big films from Hollywood loaded with Bears on the battlefield. *Gone with the Wind* may be a queer standard, yet Scarlett is not always the draw. Tom, the Yankee captain who comes to arrest Ashley is worth sitting through the whole four hours.

From Russia with Love
Fiddler on the Roof, Nicholas and Alexandra and *Dr. Zhivago*: Bears from the Russian Revolution on celluloid.

Moscow on the Hudson Robin Williams at his fuzziest

Bears of the Old Country
where the Bear heritage can be traced

The Highland Bear

Countries	England, Scotland, Ireland, Wales
"Bear"	Scottish & Gaelic "mathan"
	Welsh "arth"
Occupation	shepherd, pub bartender or ferryman
Clothes	kilt
Traditions	highland games (tossing the caber) Edinburgh Tattoo (blowing bagpipes)
Hair	red and wavy sparse and spotty beard, full bushy moustaches
Mascot	Paddington
Fun Fact	Brass plaque inspection involves standing on a reflective floor so that your superior sees only your goods and no underwear

The Alpine Bear

Countries	Germany, Switzerland, Austria
"Bear"	German "bär"
Occupation	member of an oompah band, bell ringer, wood carver, or dairy farmer
Clothes	lederhosen
Traditions	slap dancing in a beer hall
Hair	blond to light brown full bushy moustaches
Mascot	a Steiff teddy bear
Fun Fact	Yodeling is the reverse of deep throating

The Mediterranean Bear

Countries	Italy, France, Spain and Portugal
"Bear"	French "ours"
	Italian "orso"
	Spanish "oso"
	Catalan "ós"
	Portuguese "orso"
Occupation	restaurateur, chef, sommelier or Mafia
Clothes	Armani suit, Bruno Magli shoes and gold chains
Traditions	weekend in Sitges or Ibiza and then going to confession
Hair	dark brown to black notable body hair well groomed Beard and moustache
Mascot	the Bear statue in the middle of Madrid
Fun Fact	Italian Bear Actor Bud Spencer played Father Orso in _We Are Angels_. He also has done spaghetti westerns.

The Aegean Bear

Countries	Greece, Albania and Cyprus
"Bear"	Greek "arxtoz"
	Albanian "ari"
Occupation	fisherman
Clothes	apron; the Greek military men wear skirts
Traditions	plate breaking, dancing with other men, kissing other men and where do you think the term "Greek" came from?
Hair	premature salt and pepper and a constant 5 o'clock shadow
Mascot	Ursa Major, the Greek constellation
Fun Fact	The Bacchanal is the original Bear run

The Slavic Bear

Countries	Bulgaria, Romania, Slovak Republic, Former Yugoslavia and Hungary
"Bear"	Hungarian "medve" Czech "medvÆd" Slovak & Serbian "medved" Romanian "urs"
Occupation	weightlifter
Clothes	weightlifting belt and singlet
Traditions	lifting weights
Hair	light brown thin hair
Mascot	Whoever the Gold Medalist in weightlifting was from the last Olympics Or the two real bears that guard the palace in Cesky Krumlov in the Czech Republic
Fun Fact	Slovakia, Romania and Bulgaria all have handsome Bearded men on their paper money

The Eastern European Bear

Countries	Russia, Baltics, Poland and Ukraine
"Bear"	Russian "medvyed" Ukraine "beæmiæb" Polish "niedzwiedz"
Occupation	factory worker for the people, spy, military
Clothes	heavy wool coat and fur hat
Traditions	squat dancing, vodka drinking and balalaika playing
Hair	brown thick and straight goatees and heavy eyebrows
Mascot	Misha, from the 1980 Olympics in Moscow or a circus dancing bear or the real life bear depicted on the Belarus currency
Fun Fact	Poland's 10 zloty (the paper money) has a medieval Bear prince in profile who becomes a king on the 50

The Scandinavian Bear

Countries	Norway, Sweden, Denmark and Finland
"Bear"	Norwegian and Danish "bjørn" Swedish "björn" Finnish "karhu"
Occupation	whaling, oil rig worker or Viking
Clothes	pelts
Traditions	raping and plundering villages
Hair	blond hair, dark beard, full but unkempt facial hair
Mascot	a polar bear
Fun Fact	The Danish coat of arms not only has a polar bear on it, but two strapping Bear men as well

The Middle Eastern Bear

Countries	Turkey, Iraq, Armenia, Israel, Iran, Saudi Arabia and Lebanon
"Bear"	Hebrew "dov" Arabic "dub"
Occupation	nomad, Hammam proprietor, rug salesman or lawyer
Clothes	kaftan (optional yarmulke and curls for Israel)
Traditions	grease wrestling
Hair	black, thick and curly on head, face and body
Mascot	Moses
Fun Fact	David vs. Goliath was the first Bear bitch cat fight

Places with Bear in the Name

The word bear has been used throughout history as a good name for an area, town or city. Bern, Switzerland and Berlin, Germany are both named for the hairy beast. In Poland there is a district in Warsaw named Ursus. There is even a Bear Island in Ireland. According to Geographic Names Information, BEAR is used in more than 5700 places in the USA. Listing all of them would be ridiculous, and visiting them would be close to impossible. It is certain, however, that it would look good on a trick card as a place of residence. There are also so many Bear Canyons and Bear Gulches in Colorado and California that they needed to be left off of the list.

Bear, DE
Bear Creek, AL, MT & WI
Bear Creek Village, PA
Bear Dance, MT
Bear Grass Point, NC
Bear Gully Canal, FL
Bear Lake Hot Springs, ID
Bear Inlet, NC
Bear Island Beach, ME
Bear Jump, NM
Bear Lake, MI & PA
Bear Lodge Mountains, WY
Bear Mans Bluff, TX
Bear Meadow, CA
Bear Mountain, AR, KY, MA, OR
Bear Mountain Bridge, NY
Bear Paw Mountains, MT
Bear Pond Mountains, MD
Bear Rapids, MT
Bear Riffle, OR
Bear River, NS
Bear River City, UT
Bear Slough Bend, AK
Bear Spring, TN
Bear Swamp, MA

Bear Swamp Pumped Storage Lower Dam, MA
Bear Tavern, NJ
Bear Tooth Pass, WY
Bear Town, MS
Bear Trap Dam, MI
Bear Valley, CA
Bear Wallow, CO
Bearmeat Gap, GA
Bearskin Neck, MA
Beartrap Junction, WY
Beartown, KY & OH
Bearville, KY

For the Cubs
Cub Run, KY

For the Grizzlies
Grizzly Mountain, ID, OR, WY

For those who still know Latin
Ursus Lake, AK
Ursus Hill, MT
Ursine, NV
Ursina, PA

The United States of Abearica

From the redwood forest to the Gulf Stream waters, Bears are all over this country. There are, of course, the wild four-legged bears that inhabit the wilderness, but there are also the biped types that inhabit the bars and clubs.

Bear States

Seven states in the union have little-known connections to the bear. **Kentucky** and **Arkansas**: Both were known as The Bear State during frontier days due to the large population of bears in the territory. **New Mexico** and **West Virginia**: Both have a bear as the state animal: New Mexico, because this is the birthplace of Smokey the Bear and West Virginia because a poll of schoolchildren deemed it so in 1955. **California**: The state animal, a grizzly bear, is on the state seal and state flag. California was known as the Bear Republic by the Sonoma Settlers in their rebellion against Mexican rule in 1846. **Missouri**: Three bears emblazon the state seal: two large silver tips holding the state motto and a grizzly Bear on the seal itself. **Alaska**: The bear is hidden in the state flag in the form of the constellation Ursa Major.

Bears of the New World Part 2

The Bears Down Under

Not Necessarily Bears Who Bottom

Spawned from the loins of the European old countries, the Bear man is primarily thought of as an American ideal. However in another part of the world, where some Englishmen landed (by choice or as punishment) seeds for a similar Bear man were planted. Australia's rough terrain fostered a rugged outdoorsy sort of bloke that wasn't partial to the sheilas. The Australian Bear emerged.

Australia has roots as a British penal colony, established due to the overpopulation of London jails in the 18th century, and we've all heard tales of jail house romance. Prison is the best place to find a man that won't roam. So, with all those big burly convicts it is no wonder that Australia has grown into a place for a Bear population to grow, and a destination for foreign Bears to visit.

An encounter with an Aussie Bear can prove to be interesting. They are nothing like the waiters at The Outback Steakhouse. Most American Bears will meet Aussies in one of two places: online or the bar. Both are popular with Aussie Bears. Due to the Aussie's love of alcoholic intake, meeting him in the "pub" is very likely, however that would mean an 18 hour plane trip for you or him. Think coach seats: the option of meeting online becomes more appealing.

When looking for Australian Bears online, there is a good chance you will run into one or two in #bearcave on IRC but be sure to be on Undernet instead of Efnet. Also realize there is a drastic time difference. So if you don't meet any Bears from Sydney online at 2pm Eastern Standard time, that's because it's 4am there and they are most likely in bed. Not asleep mind you, but in bed nonetheless, and usually not alone.

Because Australia is an island nation, there are no real bears indigenous to the continent. They do have the Koala, however it is not a bear. The Koala is a marsupial. It has a pouch for its young like a kangaroo. Real Bears have gym bags, backpacks and book bags, but never a pouch that equates to a papoose or a diaper bag. The Koala's saving grace is that it is so damned cute. It is understandable why it is thought to be the inspiration for the

the wombat

Teddy Bear. The Wombat, a rather cute, docile oversized rat, is actually a closer relative to the bear and has become the adoptive name of certain Bear groups down under.

Bear clubs do flourish in Australia and suffer the same internal political infighting that any social organization has. The Bears, however, do make a good showing at the biggest party in Sydney, Gay and Lesbian Mardi Gras. The Bear contingency makes up one of, if not the, largest group represented in the parade.

How to Cruise in 'Strine

One arvo I was at the beat looking for a truckie to work my old fella for me. I cruised this spunky bloke that followed me into the dunny. He had on a pair of stubbies that looked like they would pop. We opted to head to the steamies to root. Turns out he was a kiwi that liked his arse worked. When we finished we both lit up some fags.

Translation: One afternoon I was lurking at a cruisy area looking for a trucker who would blow me. I met up with a sexy guy who followed me into the public men's room. He had on a pair of really tight fitting zipperless shorts and he was hard. We went to the public baths for sex. It turns out he was from New Zealand and liked to bottom. We smoked when we were done.

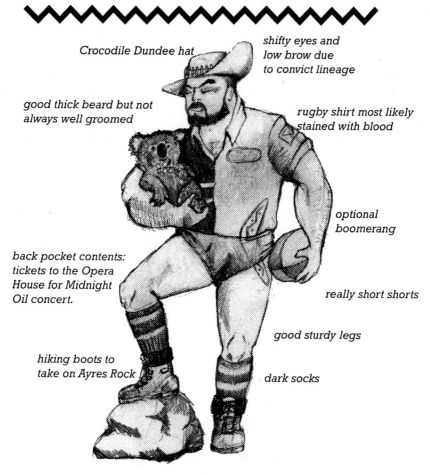

Crocodile Dundee hat

shifty eyes and low brow due to convict lineage

good thick beard but not always well groomed

rugby shirt most likely stained with blood

optional boomerang

back pocket contents: tickets to the Opera House for Midnight Oil concert.

really short shorts

good sturdy legs

hiking boots to take on Ayres Rock

dark socks

And then came the Queer Bears

The Bear Movement

As with most movements, there is no official start. Movements evolve. Gay Liberation is often thought to have started with the Stonewall Riots, but one event sparking a revolution is like saying that God snapped his fingers and Adam and Eve appeared in the Garden of Eden. Movements take a series of events to grow into something substantial, and the Bear Movement is no exception.

After WWII, when the boys came back home to be breadwinners and the women went into their June Cleaver mode, Ike took office and America became the most powerful nation in the world. The U.S. became a White Anglo Saxon Protestant male-run society. But then African Americans, being the trend setters that they are, got the ball rolling. Civil Rights of the '60's begat Women's Lib of the '70's. At the beginning of the '80's, the Village People provided the soundtrack for queers who came together to bitch about their rights. Later in the decade, the white male had to get in touch with his inner "Iron John" and become a sensitive New Age guy with the Men's Movement. The men caught between these two movements could be considered the foundation for Bears: Gay men who found unity in a masculine brotherhood.

At the same time, the fashion world was going through some trends: models started puking and there was a surge of male fashion awareness. By the time the '80's rolled around nobody wanted to look like what they looked like. Everyone started all types of makeovers and self-improvement regimens that usually involved some sort of weight loss. In this time span, hair became a fashion factor too. It grew from Eisenhower-decade crewcuts to long flowing locks of the flower children to the permed, feathered and blow-dried Sassoon styles. When gays started making some noise in the early '80's, the mainstream saw the gay male image as the twink that appeared in International Male. When hippies were growing beards to get back to a more natural man, some of them were gay (believe it or not). Not all of the natural men of the '60's evolved into corporate clones of the '80's. Some of them became Radical Faeries, a splinter group of gay men with Jesus-like looks. Sometimes involved with Wicca and always environmentally conscious, these queers showed that you could break the gay image, still be happy, and that hair, be it facial or body, was natural and good.

Then masculinity made its way back into the gay bars with the help of the Leather Community. Not all gay men were mincing about in polyester at Studio 54. Some were in darkened backrooms doing terribly wonderful things to one another. Of course afterwards they were exchanging leather-cleaning tips, but still, in the moment, they were bad-asses. All these ingredients started to add up: Gay masculine men coming together, rejecting the stereotypical image of gays; feeling comfortable with their bodies and allowing themselves to enjoy their sexuality.

The Bear Movement emerged. Big, hairy, husky gay men started forming small groups. They were open to anyone who wanted to have a good time, regardless of what they looked like. Gathering together to watch Star Trek reruns and have hot tub parties, the movement became

something of an underground cult. In its intended form, the Bear Movement was less structured and it seemed to have a sleaze factor that was undeniable. It was just a group of men who enjoyed trivial pursuits and having sex together. A lot of sex. But then it evolved and started getting away from its roots (or at least that is what some

Bears will bitch about). The Bear weekends, which were mostly about getting your rocks off, have grown into social events where old friends meet and seminars are held. Bear beauty contests that put labels on people and crown someone better than the others have become a serious competition for sash queens. Bear groups became organized, held elections and drew up bylaws. Some have even gone so far as to do charity work, community service, and become politically active.

As stated, the Bear movement is just that — a movement. It is still in its infancy and will continue to evolve and grow. And as it has had no official start, it will have no official end.

Read More About It!
If you would like to know more about the history of Bears and Bear Men, don't check out your local library unless the librarian is cute, check out **www.bearhistory.com** **(please note web site rule on page 66)**

The Bear Flag: Old Glory It Ain't!

The banner of any society is important. In this one symbol, it must embody the essence of the organization. If that is the case, then the Bear flag should be a napkin with tomato sauce on one side and a cum stain on the other. But it is not. Once the Bear movement got organized enough to form Bear clubs and write up bylaws, someone said, "Hey, we need something to put on a tee shirt so that we can be unified and segregate ourselves from the rest of the world." Oddly enough George Washington said the exact same thing to Betsy Ross. So our little Betsy Rosses set to work creating that one symbol that would exemplify Beardom.

The first design with any sort of record is that of the Front Range Bears. It was created in 1992 and used as a symbol for Bears in pride parades in Denver, San Francisco and the March on Washington in 1993. The PMS colors used are Golden- 124C, Grey- 420C, Brown- 469C, and Process Black and White.

Using a similar diagonal pattern, Seattle boasted its own interpretation of an emblem for the Bears. This one dealt more with the symbolism of color. Using the blue of the sky and the green of the grass, this flag is not seen a whole lot outside of the Northwest corridor.

The obvious design is the offshoot of the Gay Rainbow Flag. With the multicolored salute to Dorothy as a base, that emblem design became the standard for any sexual deviant group. The Leather Community uses black and blue stripes and emblazons them with a red heart. In 1995 The International Bear Brotherhood Flag was trademarked and marketed. This design is not dissimilar from the Leather Flag. The colors represent all the fur colors and nationalities of Bears throughout the world (instead of a bruise) and the heart is replaced with a paw. What is unique about this design is the marketing of it. It has found its way onto tee shirts, bumper stickers, baseball caps, watches, stained glass, quilts, floor rugs, license plates, luggage tags, buttons and pins. Oh yes, and it's available as a flag too. Betsy and George would be proud.

There are other flags that seem only to exist in cyberspace. Most variations are merely a mixing of the Rainbow Flag and the warm colors of the Bear Flags, although Bears from around the world have redesigned their own country's flags and emblazoned them with the paw print. Most notable ones come from Australia, Brazil and Canada where the paw prints have taken the place of the Union Jack, the Blue Circle and the Maple leaf.

Why a Bear and not a Gorilla?

Lives in the cool woods and is called Prince of the Forest	Lives in the hot tropical areas of the world; that means sweating and chafing
Hairy back, chest, legs and butt	Bald chest
Gentle Ben and Yogi Bear; Gentle and always after picnic baskets	King Kong and Magilla Gorilla. Not the personification one strives for, although Kong is good for size queens
Forest Rangers	Dian Fossey and Tarzan
Salmon, trout and honey	Fleas off each other's backs
Leather Bears at Play and *Bear Sex Party*	*Planet of the Apes* and *Congo*

Winnie the Pooh
Part 1 The Real Story

The original story starts with a British veterinarian, Harry Cole-bourne, who lived in Winnipeg, Canada. In 1914 he signed up as a solidier and left for Quebec by train for overseas action in WW I. On the way he stopped in White River, Ontario where he bought a black bear cub for $20.00 from a local hunter.

The cub became the mascot of Harry's regiment. In December when his unit shipped out, the cub, nicknamed Winnie after Harry's hometown,was put in the London Zoo for safekeeping. So far the story is: Bear gets picked up in train station by soldier and dumped when he has to go to work. It's not really a new story.

The Ursine Arts

or Masturbating to Masterpieces

Edouard Manet
detail from Luncheon on the Grass *1863*

Unlikely as it may seem, Bearmen have played a significant role in the arts. Bears are sensitive and compassionate with the soul of an artist. This one trait is what separates a Bear from a Neanderthal, although the amount of body hair on both is strikingly similar. Bears have a certain grace that is not that of a figure skater. It is not that delicate, but it is still deliberate and skilled. Whether it's in the well-crafted words of a novel, the bravado of belting out an aria, or the meticulous ink-drawn lines of an erotic etching, Bears have excelled as poets, painters and actors. The only realm of the arts in which a Bear is seldom seen is the ballet; that circuit belongs to screaming Nancy chorus boys. However a Bear might make an appearance at a fundraiser in a tutu. (Tulle and leotards are not kind to Bears and some folks would pay good money to see it.) It is important to remember that the Arts and Humanities are representative of the culture in a society and communicate to the ages about that society. In looking at the presence of Bearmen in the arts, it is obvious that bearded burly men have had an impact. In other words, Bears are not only found at the Museum of Natural History or the zoo; they're in libraries, art museums, theaters, cinemas and concert halls. Face it, Bears are classy!

Bears in the Visual Arts

Statuary
Bears like to touch, so the good, hard bronze from the Roman Empire or the cool marble of Greek statues are on the list of any Bear's favorite pieces of art. Also, replicas of these dress up any den and give an air of sophistication. No one has to know the statuary has been fondled while its owner was whacking off.

Roman Statuary
Hadrian **and** *Caracalla*

Popular Pieces:
Greek Statuary - Anything that has Zeus or Poseidon
Roman Statuary - Anything of Emperor Hadrian - who was bearded, brawny and gay
Rossi - Hercules and Diomede - very pornographic: two Bearded men in combat. And this is pre-WWF!

Painting Any Bear who sat through the compulsory "Art in the Dark" class for three credits their freshman year found that visually there was nothing "stimulating" until the 1500s. Oh sure, a beard here or a moustache there on a monarch, but nothing to get stiff over. For the most part artists were painting nude women. And although some of these nudes, in girth, could be Bears (check out a Rubens model) they were by no means "arousing" to the Bear that sits in the dull art lecture. That is when the undergraduate Bear starts to realize that the goateed professor is spending far too much time commenting on the torsos of Renaissance soldiers and dropping trivia like, "Did you know da Vinci was gay?" No doubt, the professor had dabbled in oils.

Erotica Seen on Grecian urns and Venetian frescos, gay men playing with one another is nothing new. Today, however, Bear men have challenged artists to draw each strand of hair on the back as well as the ass, head and pubic area. Most Bear erotic artists started out doodling muscle men at an early age. "I'm an artist" was a good excuse to stare at penises. Of course that will work when you're 15; your mother will be wondering, but it'll work. On the other hand, when you're a CPA at 35, staring at some guy's dick and saying "I'm an artist," it is just code for "I'm queer."

Bears in the Audible Arts

Where the visual lets off the audible picks up. There have been and are many Bears in the music industry. The Bear may growl but he has effectively learned to turn that growl into a sound that brings joy to the ear.

Vocal. The joining of voices is a beautiful thing and Bears have always had a presence in vocal musical groups. Traditionally the Bear is a Bass, however a Bear who wears his shorts a bit too tight and thinks he is Beverly Sills is a Tenor. Barbershop Quartets inevitably have one Daddy Bear who keeps that bass line humming. He will also have a knockout handlebar moustache and muttonchops. In any metropolitan city the Gay Men's Chorus will be dotted with beards in the Bass section. The gay chorus is for those queers who want to relive their high school chorus experience without being ostracized.

Classical. As with choral music, music without words also has been associated with Bears. Orchestras will have Bears playing tubas, trombones, and bassoons, and there will always be a beard or two in the percussion section. Bears are not just at the execution end of the music, however, but also in the composing of it. The history of composition is loaded with talented artists who had beards— most of them being Russians with almost unpronounceable names.

Rock and Roll. The advent of Rock was to go against the musical grain of the time. Bears did not make their debut in the Rock forum until the Psychedelic Era when beards appeared on hippies and flower children. Once Bears appeared, however, they stayed. It is not uncommon to see a beard in a Heavy Metal Band or a <u>Bear</u> Magazine cap on an Alternative band member.

Country. It is the one genre of music that allows a man to really pour his guts out, have facial hair, wear tight jeans and drive a pickup.

Show Tunes. It may not really be a Bear thing, but there are very few queers who do not own Barbra's Broadway Album and at least one other original cast recording. Bears also frequent Sidetracks in Chicago for Showtune night!

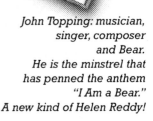

John Topping: musician, singer, composer and Bear. He is the minstrel that has penned the anthem "I Am a Bear." A new kind of Helen Reddy!

Happy Bear Song

That disjointed tune that is coming from your lover's mouth is merely a happy mindless noise telling you that he is content. Often the tune has no rhyme or reason. It is just a random selection of dum-de-dums, and hum-bumby-dums strung together that make up this odd melody. Very often the "hummer" has no idea he is even making a sound. More often than not, he does it without even thinking. This hum is perpetuated when the Bear is happy, sated, or whipping up fudge.

When Metal and Teddy Bears Collide
Nothing like a Bear clad in leather. Sure the Spice Girl heels and makeup are a bit much, but the tongue is a big hit.

The Top Ten Bearded Men in Music

Suffice it to say, most musicians have at one time or another had a beard. It's usually at that time in his career when he needs an "artistic" change. These men are rarely, if ever, seen without a beard.

10 Bryn Terfel This opera guy is best known for being mistaken for Meatloaf… Meatloaf with a beard, that is.

9 Benny Andersson Once a member of Abba, he went on to co-write the musical CHESS.

8 & 7 Tchaikovsky and Brahms The classical duo that haunt Tim Barela's *Leonard and Larry* series.

6 Kenny Rogers A killer gray beard, a song in his heart, and a roasted chicken chain named after him

5 John Philip Sousa Creator of music that many a Bear played the Sousaphone to in marching band

4 & 3 Stephen Sondheim and Hal Prince The Broadway duo that either wrote or directed modern classics of the Great White Way.

2 Barry White Soul music from a voice that makes your balls tingle

1 Jerry Garcia - Dancing Bears in rainbow colors!

The Bear as Thespian

An Introduction to Big Burly Men in Show Biz Niz

The leading man is never a Bear. At least that has been the rule for far too long. Bears are the wise-ass sidekicks or the thug villains, but rarely the hero. For the most part, though, these character actors are more impressive, more vivid and downright cuter than the chiseled-jaw main actor. Dan Blocker as *Hoss Cartwright* was always the goofy one out of the three brothers on *Bonanza*, but he's the one that was the cause for many a Bear's ruined sheets; the dream was that Sebastian Cabot, *Mr. French* on *Family Affair*, would launder those dirty sheets. Even in film, men like John Rhys-Davies played Indiana Jones's guy Friday— and maybe his guy Saturday night if Harrison Ford had any taste. The large lumbering actor has been cast as a foil to the glamourpuss in some instances. Ritch Brinkley played *Murphy Brown's* Carl the Cameraman, always fawning over Candice Bergen while thousands of guys fawned over him. Ed Asner will always be thought of as the gruff but loveable teddy bear *Lou Grant* to Mary Tyler Moore's Barbie doll-like *Mary Richards*.

But then Bears started moving from supporting roles to leads. Asner continued as *Lou Grant* in his own show. At about the same time, bearded Pernell Roberts headed up the surgery staff in *Trapper John, M.D.* A lot of queers

Funny Bears

Mike McShane *Who's Line is it Anyway*
Dom DeLuise *Any Burt Reynolds Film*
Jeremy Piven *Ellen*
Kevin Smith *Dogma*
Rob Reiner *This is Spinal Tap*
Kevin James *The King of Queens*
Jack Weston *The Four Seasons*
Ned Beatty *Deliverance*
(OK, it's not a comedy but you know it makes you smile!)

tuned into that show to watch Gregory Harrison, but Pernell was far sexier.

Daddy Bears in Show Biz

Noah Beery Jr.- *Rockford Files*
Raymond Burr- *Ironside*
Burl Ives- *Cat on a Hot Tin Roof*
Wilford Brimley - *In & Out*
Robert Prosky - *Veronica's Closet*

Bear actors are now looked upon as leading men. This is most likely because scripts have gotten more realistic. The world is not full of just pretty boys, so why should they be the focus of everything? Blue-collar types like *Ralph Kramden* (one of the non-pretty boys in early TV) have come back into vogue. *Dan Conner*, played by John Goodman, was the new Bear of suburbia who replaced Ward Cleaver. He even sported a Chicago Bears shirt now and then. One season he had a beard, although co-starring with *Roseanne* he may not have been the man in the family. *Brian Dennehy* at his bearish best commands the screen as the lead in *The Belly of an Architect.* With his scruffy beard and girth, he has pride as, draped only in a towel, he takes the vapors at an Italian spa. (This is an inspiring image to any Bear.) Given the chance, Bears perform well. *Dennis Franz* collected back-to-back Emmys for portraying Andy Sipowicz in the controversial *NYPD Blue*. If only it was *his* butt shot that opened the series and not David Caruso's.

Other Bearish Thespians

furry pecs
> Patrick Warburton
> Alec Baldwin

moustache
> Sam Elliot
> Tom Selleck

beards sometimes
> Ed Harris
> Robert DeNiro
> Tom Skerritt
> Kurt Russell
> James Brolin (queer points for being in *Pee Wee's Big Adventure* and romantically linked with Barbra)

bear built
> James Gandolfini

And now a word from our sponsor: *Cliff ,the IHOP guy. He's burly and the spokesman for pancakes— He just may give Al a run for his money.*

Queer Bear Milestones in Acting

1971- <u>Women in Love</u>. Oliver Reed and Alan Bates, both with ample fur, wrestle naked in an English drawing room. It is manly and playful, but the homosexual overtones cannot be denied. The rest of the film is very arthouse, and yes, you do see dick.

1994- <u>Northern Exposure</u>. Ron Bantz and Eric Hillman play Doug Ballard and Don McManus, the first gay couple on TV to have a commitment ceremony, and one of them was a Bear. They own one of the local Bed and Breakfasts ....at least they weren't florists.

1996- <u>Wings</u>. Abraham Benrubi plays the beefy gay son of Roy Biggins, R.J. In a later episode R.J. brings home his boyfriend to meet dad. Abe shatters the gay stereotype into tiny bite-size pieces and lands himself a prime role in NBC's smash <u>ER</u>. Unfortunately in the latter show, he's straight.

1996- <u>The Bird Cage</u>: The American non-musical version of *La Cage Aux Folles* stars Nathan Lane and Robin Williams as a South Beach couple. The Bear factor on their lifestyle as Drag Queen and club owner are low, but Lane has the roundness and Williams has the body hair to attract Bears to the theater.

1997- <u>In and Out</u>: You just gotta giggle when Wilford Brimley says "I'm Howard's father, and I'm gay!"

1997- <u>Love! Valour! Compassion!</u>: Stout Jason Alexander plays the cuddly queen in this Terrence McNally classic.

2 TV BEAR ICONS

Grizzly Adams In the late '70's, while the rest of the world was getting ready to clad themselves in leisure suits, NBC was bringing out the buckskin. Their hit _Little House on the Prairie_ had been a ratings grabber for three years. Bears were tuning in, not for the sugary sweet stories about the Ingalls family, but to see Victor French as _Mr. Isaiah Edwards_ and Merlin Olsen as _Jonathan Garvey_, two bearded men who took on the frontier. But in 1977, there was a new husky pioneer in the wilderness. _The Life and Times of Grizzly Adams_, Wednesdays at 8pm (EST), made Dan Haggerty a household name and a masturbatory fantasy for little boys with a bent for facial hair. He had the fullest beard since Santa Claus that outlined the blinding white teeth of a killer smile. His tanned skin covered his bulky frame and complemented the twinkle in his eye. Alas, his time slot competition was tough. Where he reigned in Big Sky country, the Bradfords from _Eight is Enough_ ruled suburbia, and the Evans family of _Good Times_ dealt with the inner city. _The Life and Times of Grizzly Adams_ was canceled. There were rumors that Dan's beard had been burned off in a bizarre flaming drink accident (the lesson is only drink beer). If it did, it grew back by 1982 when the made-for-TV movie _The Capture of Grizzly Adams_ aired. Even though the title has porn story written all over it, it was not. Dan's face again filled the dreams of little Bears everywhere.

It should be noted that although Dan is primarily known for Grizzly Adams, he has also portrayed other butch acting parts. He was a stunning but shaved muscle man in _Muscle Beach Party_ and a bare chested, leather vested biker in the wacky queer biker romp _The Pink Angels_.

Black Bears in Show Biz

James Avery
LL Cool J
Michael Clarke Duncan
John Amos
Ving Rhames
Forest Whitaker
Ed Bradley
Mr. T
Sinbad
James Earl Jones
Barry White
George Clinton
Ernie Hudson (it's the _OZ_ thing)

sketch inspired by theatre illustrator, bearded Al Hirshfeld

Al Borland Max Baer as *Jethro Bodeen* may very well have been the first on TV to don a plaid shirt, blue jeans and work boots and call it fashion, but he never mastered the look like Al does. *Al Borland*, played by Richard Karn, was slated to be nothing more than a minor sidekick to Tim Allen's tool man Tim Taylor on *Home Improvement*. Modeled after the "master-craftsman-cum-helper" on many house renovation shows, Al is now a pivotal character in the show's storyline. Richard has molded the character into the epitome of Beardom in terms of looks and sensibilities. He is strong, yet tender; he is passionate, yet even tempered; he can tell the difference between "horizon sunset" and

"melon" when it comes to paint colors; *and* his butt looks good in jeans. He works that ensemble like Jethro never could. And he comes with a tool belt: he knows how to accessorize! Al is everything a Bear could want in a man, except one thing. He's not gay. Nor is Richard Karn.

Did Richard realize he was going to be the heartthrob of many hairy men? As Al might say, "I don't think so, Tim." The unexpected sex symbol, Richard knows that he has a Bear following and has accepted a membership as an honorary Bear with a New England Bear club. Tim Allen discussed it on Regis and Kathie Lee. (It is rumored *Bear* magazine sent an issue to Ms. Gifford to visually explain to her what Bears are.) Richard has done more than Al. His first commercial work was doing a beer ad for Michelob (so he again sneaks into the hearts of Bears). He has a son (who will no doubt grow up to be as woofy as his dad) and is married to Trudi Riche. Advice to her: Don't bring Richard near Chicago over Memorial Day!

Cable Bears

Looking for Bears on TV? You'll most likely find them on the following channels:

Discovery Channel: There are home improvment shows and archae-ology shows.

HGTV: Paul James.

Animal Planet: Real Bears and Zookeepers. Woof.

Food Network: Bears that found their way to the kitchen and Iron Chef.

TNT: WCW Monday Nitro!

Travel Channel: Bears from around the world.

Animated Bears

Bluto or Brutus
Beast (of Beauty and the)
Beast (of the Xmen)
Dr. Quest
Wolverine
Taz
Pops (of Speed Racer)
Yosemite Sam
Duke Phillips
South Park's Chef
and The Simpsons
(not really any Bears on the show, but a lot of big hairy guys seem to like 'em!)

Thespian Bears of the Illegitimate Screen

As seen, there is a horde of Bear types in the entertainment field, however only a handful can claim the moniker of Bear: he who is *horny* as well as heavy and hairy. Sure, he will be seen at the Cineplex when buying tickets or humming show tunes on his way past the Marquis Theatre, but he can also be seen on T.V. Thanks to the porn industry Bears have found an acting forum that shows off their best attributes: a fuzzy ass and a skilled tongue in video porn. The most important thing in Bear porn is that there is no plot— just sex. You can actually forego watching these men struggling to convey some Stanislavsky inner emotion and just get right to naked hairy men rolling around with each other and a money shot.

Ten things on a video box that's a good indication it won't be a good sleazy Bear type video

1 "All Asian Cast"
2 "Babe-on-Babe Action"
3 "From the Pages of International Male"
4 "Beverly Hills" somewhere in the title
5 "High School Memories"
6 Jeff Stryker
7 Catalina
8 Spandex biker pants
9 Chicks with Dicks
10 Surfboards

NAME	ERA	GAY	HAIRY			CUT	UN CUT	TOP	BOT- TOM	PECULIARITIES
			CHEST	BACK	BUTT					
Bruno	70's	X	X		X		X			one of the first bearded porn stars
Ron Jeremy	70's		X	X	X		X	X		straight, but a gay following
Moose	80's	X	X	X	X	X		X		non-bearded
Al Parker	80's	X				X	X	X	X	underwent foreskin restoration
Steve Kelso	90's	X	X			X		?	?	mostly solo work. website Hairway to Steven
AJ	90's	X	X			X		X	X	fun handlebar mustache
Buster	90's	X	X			X			X	shudders after he shoots
Jack Radcliffe	90's	X	X	X	X		X	X		plays with his nipples

Bears of Literature

English Literature 101 (like Art History 101) usually had one good thing going for it: the professor. Very often this is the prototypical romantic view of the college professor. He has a full, distinguished, salt-and-pepper beard. His balding head is exposed in summer but hidden under a tweed hat during the academic year. He has gold, circular glasses that cover his deep brown eyes accented with crow's feet. His sports coat has suede patches on the elbows, and an argyle vest covers his tummy. He smokes a pipe and is often seen in discussion with students in the smoking lounge. He looks like Sean Connery from Indiana Jones and the Last Crusade and he is the only reason you read anything other than the text for your PASCAL class. But he is not the only Bear that is found in the world of arts and letters. Bookstores and libraries hold a plethora of stories that you don't have to download to find hairy beefy men. The Bear man has been the subject of only a few books in either erotica, humor or sociology. It is not uncommon, however, to find Bears sprinkled throughout the pages of literature. Even some authors who were around long before there was a Bear movement have had Bear qualities. As for the college professor— keep your eyes peeled in the stacks at the library. That's where he likes to cruise.

While in the library, check out these authors in the card catalogue.

Ernest Hemingway, the grand daddy of bearish writers. "Papa" had it all. He had a beard, loved to drink, and was terribly butch— however he did

The two books that solely examine the phenomenon of gay men who call themselves Bears are The Bear Book, *by Les Wright, PhD, a sociological look at the bear community, how it came to be and who Bear men are, and* The Bear Cult, *an art book that is a collection of photographs of Bear men, taken by Chris Nelson. Both should be in the library of any man who thinks he is ursine and shelved next to a copy of* The Bear Handbook.

have a house in Key West loaded with cats, so it does make one wonder. Annually, there is a Hemingway look-a-like contest in Key West so if you are into Daddy types this may be the event you've been waiting for.

American Legends

The Bear man holds a special place in American mythology. They embody the American ideal and, thanks to the U.S. Post Office, Bears had a chance to lick the men that were part of a few bedtime stories. **Paul Bunyan**- the giant who could swing an ax and clear a forest and most likely hosted the Lumberjacks square dance ball. **Pecos Bill**, The American Tarzan was raised by wolves in the southwest, rode his horse Widow Maker and followed the Gay Rodeo Circuit. **Mighty Casey** is the classic version of the big league hitter, who struck out at the big game and had to endure hot locker room sex as part of his punishment. And **John Henry**, the steel driving man that beat the machine. His story proves that a man is better than a vacu-suck anyday.

Herman Melville. He was more of a Bear than he may have realized. He had a "relationship" with Nathaniel Hawthorne (House of The Seven Gables) and wrote about a tyrannical captain and his sailor. The homoerotic overtones cannot be denied. And he gave us Moby Dick; a name that has made seventh graders giggle since it was written.

Walt Whitman was a horny poet with a beard and a thing for the working "rude illiterate" class man. In other words, he liked 'em big and stupid. Walt's personal notebooks are filled with accounts of his sundries and peccadilloes. Apparently he worked the streets of New York better than Pacino in Cruising. And, according to *The Simpsons*, Walt is buried in Springfield.

John Irving is not a bear per se, but his earlier works have similar motifs that connect in some ways to beardom: There are dancing bears, bear costumes, wrestling, nurses (common Bear occupation) and Wilford Brimley in the movie version of Hotel New Hampshire.

Clive Cussler. Any of his books have the dashing-yet-rugged Dirk Pitt, the ex-Navy oceanographer-cum-James Bond. Dirk sometimes has a beard, works for a man with a red Van Dyke, hangs out with an Italian body builder, but regrettably, always gets the girl.

NEWS FLASH:
Bears in the Electronic Press

When looking for up to date Bear information that your local fag rag won't cover, click on to *www.bearpress.com*. This electronic newspaper is chock full of current information and pretty charts, just like USA Today! And it comes with less bitchiness than the BML.

Periodicals

Let the straight guys have the S.I. Swimsuit Issue. Big hairy guys have their own publications that satisfy their lust. BEAR and AMERICAN BEAR are the premier magazines that help many a Bear man soil his boxer shorts. Although they have similarities, like the fact that they publish Bear event photos months after the event, they differ in some ways too. The chart below compares them to the straight porn standards.

what's in conunon	BEAR	AMERICAN BEAR
PLAYBOY	1st on the playing field. Polished Models	Glossy paper Slick graphics Health Column
PENTHOUSE	Models apt to play with toys and may have implants	Pushed into territory and demographic to provide men with an alternative to the only game in town
HUSTLER	Good dose of Humor: Shits and Giggles	Theme layouts eg. locker room, Wizard of Oz, kitchen fun
SWANK	The Butt Hole Shot on the level of showing pink	Attainable models that you very well may have tricked with.

Winnie the Pooh Part 2 The Milne Version

Winnie became a popular attraction at the London Zoo, especially to a small boy called Christopher Robin Milne. His mother Daphne gave him a small stuffed bear he named Edward when he was younger, but at age 5 when he first saw Winnie at the London Zoo, he renamed his stuffed bear Winnie the Pooh. The Pooh comes from the name of a swan he befriended on a "holiday in the countryside." His father, A.A., noted how attached Chistopher was to Winnie the Pooh and wrote the stories of their adventures together. He formed Pooh into the cuddly, loveable, always hungry bear we now associate with the traits of Bear men. He also created his playmates: Piglet (the flustered drama queen), Tigger (caffeine addiction) Eeyore (the downer), Owl (Ms. Know it all), Rabbit (the hausfrau with a Martha Stewart fixation) and Kanga and Roo (the unwed mother and bastard child).

Finding Bears in the Real World

There are plenty of places in the world to stumble over Bears, but here are a few places that have or have had facial hair phobia.

AAA The Automobile Club of America's policy of no beards was part of a celebrated case where a man was hired with a beard, went through training with a beard, and only after he started the job was told to shave. He quit and sued.

Cincinnati Reds Marge Schott, the queen of open-minded thinking, had always had a policy that her boys wouldn't have facial hair. In 1999 Marge saw the light and repealed the rule.

Disney For a company that was founded by a man with a moustache, Disney has had a problem with facial hair. Beards are permitted only on men employed in the Production Studio, Feature Animation or Imagineering, the creative arm of this multimillion-dollar company. Not until early 2000 has Disney allowed the "squeaky clean" image of a Cast Member (a Disney employee) to be compromised with facial hair. This has changed. Moustaches adhering to a certain style and length can now be seen under the noses of anyone working at Disney. Although you'll find beards in a Disney flick (Zeus in both *Hercules* and *Fantasia*, Stromboli in *Pinocchio*, King Trident in *The Little Mermaid*, *Aladdin*'s Genie, *Beauty's* Beast and six out of the seven Dwarfs) you still won't find one letting you on the boat at *Pirates of the Caribbean*.

Domino's Only until recently could you expect that delivery boy from Domino's to show up with a full chin of hair, partially due to a former African-American employee of Domino's suing the company when he was fired for not adhering to the nationwide no-beard policy. He claimed that he suffered from pseudofolliculitis barbae ("PFB"), a skin condition that often makes shaving difficult and painful, and is not uncommon among African-American males. According to the plaintiff, the no-beard policy was discriminatory. After a few rounds in court and appeals, the verdict was that Domino's may keep their no-beard policy with only a slim window of exception for medical reasons. Since the time of that verdict Domino's reversed their stand on beards by allowing facial hair, however nothing precludes them from requiring the beards to be neatly trimmed, cleaned and at a specified length.

A Bear Market is not the local pick-up bar but a financial phrase used for dealers who sell a stock, believing it will lower in value before delivery, thus making a profit. The dealer is "The Bear." The stock sold is "Bear Skin." The term is old English.

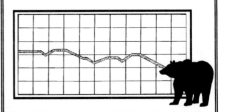

The Fantasy Bear Job vs. The Real Bear Job

Lumberjack *Related fields* Logger Fisherman	The great wooded out-doors and the possibility of roughhousing in the bunk house	**Management** *Related fields:* CPA or Under-writer	The fluorescent-lit cubi-clized indoors and the possibility of advancing to the marketing department
Forest Ranger *Related fields:* Military, Cop	Taking care of woodland creatures, and the possi-bility of randy campers that need to be taught a lesson	**Nurse** *Related fields:* Home Care Specialist	Taking care of bedridden creatures and the possibil-ity of sheet cake at the nurses station
Construction Worker *Related fields:* Welder Plumber Handyman	Working on the building before the AC is installed and the possibility of your co-worker straining a muscle and needing a rub down	**Interior Designer** *Related fields:* Graphics Web Site Designer	Making trips to the build-ing to look at the construc-tion workers and the pos-sibility that the construction team will stay on schedule
Truck Driver *Related fields:* Longshoreman Taxi Driver	Hauling goods in a big rig across the US and the possi-bility of meeting some good buddies at the truck stop	**Waiter** *Related fields:* Bartender at TGIFridays	Hauling food on big trays across a crowded dining room and the possibility of the culinary team asking you to sample new dishes
Mechanic	Getting your overalls greasy working beneath the hood of a car and the possibility of the truck driver coming in for a tune up	**Computer Technician** *Related fields:* Programmer MAC Support Web Master	Getting ink on your short-sleeve dress shirt because you wouldn't wear a pock-et protector and the possi-bility of finding all the hid-den stuff in Windows 98
Cable Guy *Related fields:* Phone Guy Meter Reader	The possibility of installing cable at some Bear's house, and he invites you to stay for the WWF pay-per-view	**Medical Technician** *Related fields:* EMT	The possibility of rushing to a Bear's house because he's choking on a chicken wing while watching pay-per-view.
Porn Star at Brush Creek Media	Providing entertainment to horny guys and the possibility of having your pick of the Bears at a Bear event, because you're autographing your video	**School Teacher** *Related fields:* Librarian Camp Coun-selor	It becomes a porn story only if you're the wrestling coach, and there is a hairy custodian that comes to your office to fix the show-er head despite the possi-bility of being indicted.

Bear Quiz 1
The Bears Around Us

match the Bear-related quote with its origin

1. *"And every last inch of me's covered with hair"*
2. *"He's such a hairy behemoth," she said, "dumb as a box of hammers but he's such a handsome guy"*
3. *"A Burly Man is Tough, A Burly Man is Rough And when I get a Burly Man I never get enough!"*
4. *"Just say, WOOF!"*
5. *"There is many a man that hath more hair than wit"*
6. *"Sometimes you get the Bear, sometimes the Bear gets you, but always dress for the hunt"*
7. *"A Bear? Bears are sweet. Besides you ever see a bear with forty-foot feet?"*
8. *"I'm not fat! I'm festively plump"*
9. *"Exit, pursued by bear"*

A. *Stage Direction Shakespeare's A Winter's Tale*

B. *From ABC's Fridays*

C. *Shakespeare's Comedy of Errors*

D. *Gaston Disney's Beauty and the Beast*

E. *The Witch Into the Woods*

F. *The Motto of The Adventurer's Club*

G. *Jill Sobule, I Kissed a Girl*

H. *Eric Cartman, South Park*

I. *Anonymous Tee Shirt*

CHAPTER TWO

KNOWING THE BEARS IN THE ZOO

how to identify the breed
or
"Funny, you don't look gay"

Growing Up as a Bear

Even though cubs now entering adolescence have the support of the relatively young Bear community, it is still a bitch growing up outside the norm. In the past, Bears have had to resort to unconventional means of support from otherwise non-Bear communities to come to terms with their bulk, hair and gayness. The Generation X Bears have little need for old Rosalind Russell films because of the 90's onslaught of queer media. (Say to any cub with a scrappy goatee, "Judy," and his response will be "Tenuta," not "Garland.") Today's cubs may not realize what it was like growing up as a Bear in the 50's, 60's, 70's, or 80's, so here's a history lesson for them.

Class of '62 - As a Bear you were either on the football team or the marching band (both have queer overtones to them). You had a crewcut, were a member of the AV squad and your nickname was Buzz. Kennedy launched the Space Program and that had you thinking how cool it would be to be an astronaut and explore the outer limits (it's that Sci-Fi thing). You took Metal Shop 1, 2 and 3 because you liked the teacher (He was a Bear and you just didn't realize you were gay at the time). After high school you force yourself into a "straight" world and even marry a woman (it didn't last and you're still paying alimony). Years later when you did come out, it was with a vengeance!

Class of '72 - You had to press against the pew in front of you to try to push down your erection that sprung up during the bearded priest's sermon when you were 13. You also had no problems growing a goatee that same year and earned the nickname Fuzz Ball. You seriously wanted to go to Woodstock, not necessarily for the music, but because you heard there would be a mud pit. One Saturday

night, you found yourself at an orgy and enjoyed that hairy college guy better than the girl you were dating. This is when you realized you could be gay (or maybe it was the pot. The next week you realize, it wasn't the pot). You develop a thing for Jerry Garcia. Your father wondered why you signed up for Home Ec Classes and have a hobby of leather craft. You watch *Star Trek* for the harmony of cultures. After graduation you consider moving to Canada.

Class of '82 - As a little boy your sister gets the Barbie Dreamhouse, which you love to peer into. You insist that your G.I. Joe with real hair and beard (not form injected plastic like Ken) is better suited to dwell in that house and not that damned blonde. By age 12 you and your mother are shopping in the Sears boys department for corduroy Toughskins, Size: husky. Later that year, the noise that came from the cords rubbing between your thighs disappears and is replaced by flesh starting to come through the threadbare material. You had a perm or wings and spent too much time on your hair, but so did all the guys. Beards weren't fashionable so you didn't even try, although your moustache came in good enough to screw up your yearbook photo. You spent about half of your college education fund at SpacePort on the weekends and all you wanted for Christmas was the new Journey album and an Atari 5200. The fact that you might be queer came into your head the day *A Chorus Line* played in your town and you saw it on a field trip. The fact you might be gay occurred to your friends when you had been playing *Eddie* for weeks at Rocky Horror and all of a sudden wanted to play *Janet*. Comic books are tantamount to pornography, and a wet dream about Wolverine is not uncommon.

The Bear Cub
Ursus younges

All species of Bears must start out as a cub. Even those who do not blossom into Beardom until late in life were at one time a wide-eyed young cub. The bravado and energy that is exuded in youth seem ten times more potent when combined with the fun loving attitude of a Bear. The young cub is often found discovering his world by playing and getting into mischief. Being reared by a dominant mother Bear and a father that has gone off to the salmon run for extended periods of time, a cub is brought up in a world that is filled with lessons learned mostly through trial and error. A cub's emergence into the world of grown-up Bears is by happenstance.

Young Bears, young twinks and young otters (sometimes all three traveling together) will venture into the realm of the gay bar. The notorious watering holes of the adult male Bears have such a specific following that they have very relaxed ID checks at the door and rarely have a cover charge to get in. This plays on two of the cub's attributes: the readiness to obtain liquor while still being underage, and a student budget that limits him from going to the trendy establishments that charge 5 bucks at the door with a two drink minimum. Where attitude is often the prerequisite for admittance and acceptability in this type of bar, young gay men do not often exude attitude while trying to flash a fake ID. Often the young gays will find the Bear bar the most accepting. Not unlike a debutante at her cotillion, the cub will make an entrance into the bar for the first time and all heads will turn. "Fresh Meat" is often heard muttered about the bar. The cub quickly figures out how to play at the watering hole with the other Bears. He learns to order a beer, drink shots and develop his appreciation for the older man. Sometimes the cub is searching for his daddy or sometimes he is looking for a playmate, but he is always looking for trouble. The cub will eventually grow into one of the species of Bears, but will always be a cub at heart. Some men obsessed with youth will try to maintain their cub status well into their early 40s, but they are pushing it. An old cub can be a sad character and will always be a bottom.

Eastpak book bag contents:
2 pillow packs of Wet, condoms, last
month's Advocate, cock ring, journal,
sweat shorts, Smashing Pumpkins
and Pet Shop Boys CDs

baseball cap

hair gel on top
shaved (#1 guard)
on sides

scruffy goatee at best

freedom rings

no hair
on ass
or back

Black Bear
Pride tee shirt

startings of a belly

shaved groin

Joe Boxers

faded Silver
Tab Levis

tattoo and
a piercing

sneakers

contents of pocket:
pack of Bubble Tape,
phone number of cute
Bear in Spanish class,
$1.83 in change

The Black Bear
Ursus americanus

The Black Bear has many names: Cinnamon Bear (when he is brownish), Glacier Bear (bluish color), Master, Leather Boy, Hairy Beggar, Mr. Bear and Outrageous Nuisance, but mostly he wants to be called "Sir."

His appearance is intimidating, and if met in the forest he should be treated as any wild animal. If, however, he is met in the darkened corner of the Eagle or in some back alley, his demeanor will most likely be amorous.

The Black Bear is native thoughout North America and is most commonly found at biker runs and Harley shops. At both he is likely to be window shopping only.

He will also be found in the bedding section of Macy's. He is partial to Percale. He is the urban Bear. He is happiest when on his back. Although he seems to be the one in control, he often wants to be told what to do. His loyalty is odd because he often wants to couple but has the potential to be a co-dependent.

head contains all the lyrics to Gentlemen Prefer Blonds

severe style on the muzzle

Body hair tufts from under black vest and above the ass crack

AIDS ribbon among Bear run pins

harness or optional black tee shirt

a red hanky in the back pocket

small hands (red hanky, you know)

Silver ring on nipple(s)

Fur: black, soft and dense for insulation

ball stretcher

Always a brownish face. Sometimes a patch or a V shape on chest

contents of pocket: Hello Kitty key ring with key to the cycle and to the apartment, poppers

boots of leather heels of helium

The Brown Bear
Ursus arctos

More commonly called a Grizzly or Kodiak, the Brown Bear can weigh in at 725 lbs. Most of it is muscle. His habitat ranges from Alaska, where he is called Aklak by Eskimos, to Garth and Reba concerts where he is told to sit down because he's blocking the view. His territory is far and wide throughout North America, Eurasia and to any city that is hosting the Gay Rodeo.

Not necessarily a real cowboy, his markings denote him as one. He has spent hours learning the Tush Push and squeezing into his jeans. He has a good sense of humor, a degree in chemical engineering, and more Country and Western CDs than the local DJ. His sex drive is good, but mating season is only after his mate proves he can follow doing the Texas Two-step.

large hat

hair thinning on top but full muzzle

groomed but not styled

analog Timex watch with brown leather band

a plaid shirt

hanky for blowin', not cruisin'

large belt buckle

distinguishable hump

Skoal in back pocket

Wrangler Jeans still a deep blue

fur: brown, moderately long mane at back of head

smallish feet

sometimes a white collar on grizzly cubs

distinguishable heel on cowboy boot

The Sloth Bear
Melurus ursinus

The Sloth Bear is perhaps the oldest form of Bear. He is natural with little grooming. Sloths are unkempt and scraggly looking, but they sure are fun. Rudyard Kipling based Baloo, from his *Jungle Book*, on this Bear because he is also known as the Jungle Joker. T.C. Smudge bases his drawings on this Bear because of their innate sex appeal. Sloth Bears are also known for their large lower lip and the absence of two front teeth. Although thought to have been bruised and lost in a bar fight, this arrangement in his mouth enables him to expertly suck termites from dead wood or suck wood until he's dead. He is found in Eurasia, head shops and Sedona, Arizona. His hair is long, straight and sometimes matted. The muzzle looks very ZZ Top. He often has a white marking on his chest or grease under his finger nails. Unlike the Black Bear, a Sloth Bear knows his way around a motorcycle.

pale skin

glazed look in eyes

colored bandana

long, straight, coarse, shaggy, unkempt on head and muzzle

stash in pocket

key ring with bottle opener

grey snout

Harley rings

chain from belt loop to wallet

dull black, white or cream V or Y on chest

long, straight, coarse, shaggy, unkempt and matted. Under legs and belly almost bare

jeans bought in '92 and only washed 7 times

The Spectacled Bear
Tremarctos ornatos

The complete opposite of the Sloth Bear is the Spectacled Bear. There is little known about these Bears because they are very shy. They are not the Jungle Joker, but instead a cautious species that live in remote areas of the world like the Andes and Cyberspace. They do not hibernate because they are net surfing till 5 am. One of their regular hangouts is the #bearcave on IRC, mostly because these Bears are smart. They are the techno Bears. They understand the Internet and they have web pages. They have gold rings around their eyes and wear glasses, hence the name. Their hair is thick, clean and shiny, and it could be gelled, but most likely not. Because these Bears are so remote, very often they miss the latest fashion trend.

starting to bald

glasses and smallish eyes

good full beard that needs trimming and shaping

short sleeve dress shirt, wrinkled

Uniball pens, Bics and one from the Sheraton

digital watch

yellowish line on face causing rings around eyes looking like spectacles

white patch on chest

Apple Powerbook

fur: jet black, long, shaggy, thick and shiny

Dockers size 42 Length 30

Nike's all the time

The Sun Bear
Helartos malyanus

The Sun Bear is the smallest member of the Bear family and is the most endangered. He is also known as Dog Bear due to his size and Honey Bear because he has an affinity for the sticky substance in his diet. He has been called Kevin, Jason or Kyle. The Sun Bear is also closely related to Twinks. The difference is the presence of body hair and good legs (often developed in a step aerobics class). His body is adorned with a yellowish crest or a gold chain. He is the most bejeweled of the Bears, and often wears more than one ring on each hand or hoop earrings.

Native to Eurasia, Golds Gym and the local tanning salon, the Sun Bear is continually working on his physique. He is a Sun Bear by choice and works at it. If he did not, he would balloon up. His butt is round, but not necessarily tight.

Adaptability to his environment is his strong suit.

He can fit in well at a Pretty Boy bar in Key West or the leather bar in Berlin. He has developed a long tongue and nails for foraging honey and grubs and for his own pleasure, and possibly his mate's. He is always wary of his food intake and tries not to indulge, however Movie Theatre Nachos and Häagen-Dazs are his weaknesses.

His mating habits are often with non-Bears but rarely will it last longer than a few weeks. Call waiting has been blamed for many a breakup with Sun Bears.

hair is unnaturally blonde, or at least lightened

stud earing

gold chain

closed cropped hair and muzzle

good, thick body fur

gold and silver bracelets, more than one

silver tips on ears and muzzle

possibility of girly hips

fur: short, smooth and dense, glossy coal black

contents of pocket: receipt from Chinese restaurant, keys to condo and Wrangler

thick, sturdy legs

yellowish crescent mark on chest

grey, heavy, wool socks slumped down over Wolverine workboots

The Giant Panda
Ailuropoda melanoleuca

It is always in contention whether or not the Giant Panda is a true Bear. He has the size, shape and appetite of a Bear, but may be closer to the raccoon or female illusionist. Their markings have labeled them "The Parti-Colored Bear." "Big Guy" is often an affectionate name given to him. He has a cuddly appearance and does not hibernate, meaning he can be found at the cruisy rest area at 4 am. The body of a Giant Panda is short and stout, barrel-like. Unlike other Bears, his forepaw has a makeshift opposable thumb. This has developed for holding bamboo and for masturbation. He is known to have a small "s" shaped penis which is not like any other Bear. Giant Pandas do not growl but instead bleat and whine in a higher pitch. Without the beard a Giant Panda could easily slip into being a Drag Queen.

clothes are usually baggy if he wears them at all

top of the head compensates for what lacks below

sparse beard

very little body hair

fur: coarse, wooly and extremely dense

Pandas like to be naked as often as possible, yet their skin is fish belly white

black patches over the eyes and the ears

bath sheet

the legs are also black

thick ankles

The Asiatic Black Bear

Selenarctos thibetanus

Said to be the most bizarre of the ursine species, The Asiatic Black Bear is also known as the Moon Bear or the Formosa Bear. They are, of course, found in East Asia and electronics conventions. He is not hairy and will grouse about not being able to grow proper facial hair. What hair he does have is glossy jet black, straight and spikey, yet very soft. His head appears round but that could be the hair cut. Flat tops are not uncommon, and the texture lends itself to the cut. Unlike the American Black Bear, he has shorter and thinner legs.

These Bears are easily trained due to an outstanding learning capability and will normally score over 1300 on the SATs. Many would say that he is not a Bear, but he aspires to be one because he loves and admires the American Ideal Bear. The wildness of Western Bears appeals to this Bear of the conservative East. Often dressing in American styles, he will still keep his fetishes hidden, sometimes wearing a ball strecher to a business luncheon. But the Far East is also a place of mystery, and some say the fluids of the Asiatic Black Bear are good for medicinal purposes. Luckily the extraction of those fluids is not necessarily painful.

jet black hair —very straight

conservative white shirt

weak facial hair

harness underneath

girth is in the belly

Casio digital watch

thin legs - no hair

fur: jet black, thick, shiny and soft

shoes will come off - socks most likely won't

The popularity of hairy bear type men can be seen in the Japanese porn book **GMen**. Beautifully drawn comics that are like Anime illustrate this journal. However all the penises are silhouetted in accordance with Japanese law.

The Polar Bear
Ursus maritimus

Whether called Nanook by the Eskimos or Daddy by the cubs, the Polar Bear is the largest carnivore on land. (That's one who eats meat.) His fur covering appears white but it's really transparent. It converts the sun's rays into heat which is handy since Polar Bears are found in the chilly Arctic North or Antique stores with the air conditioning set on 63 to preserve the wood of the 18th century Chippendale dresser. Living close to the North Pole, his appearance is similar to Santa Claus, except he is rarely dressed in red. He prefers pastels...or leather if the occasion is right. His job is his second career, and it allows him to take mini vacations to most Bear events. His room is often the suite and sometimes has a floral bouquet. He has well-developed shoulders and four inches of blubber in his rump (that comes from his first career as an executive sitting on his butt). He has an elongated neck which equates to a deep throat. He is often mature and older than his friends at the bar. His age is an asset and often other Bears eventually become Polar Bears when their fur starts to grey. Polar Bears have been in a relationship for at least 5 years, but that does not preclude him from playing around.

very straight nose

elongated neck

short hair, if any, on top of head

a white collar

full white or salt-and-pepper beard

twinkle in the eyes

pinky ring with initials of lover

full belly

rolled sleeve to show off hairy forearms

madras tie left over from preppy days

Weejuns

Being A Bear Is Not An Excuse

Words for Fat

ample
beefy
big boned
brawny
bulky
buoyant
burly
chunky
corpulent
cushy
dumpy
festively plump
five by five
fleshy
fluffy
hefty
husky
meaty
portly
pudgy
roly-poly
rotund
roomy
(A la Hannibal Lecter)
Rubenesque
squat
stocky
stout
strapping
stubby
sturdy
zaftig

Grooming is an essential part of life, and although Bears seemingly have a laissez-faire attitude about being well kept, the truth is far from that. Good hygiene habits means bathing and scrubbing with soap. Your lover may like that funky man-stink in your hole, but your co-workers may not appreciate the stench radiating from your cubicle. Your beard is something to be proud of, so keep it well conditioned and controlled. Any landscaper will tell you that there is more maintenance on keeping a jungle looking good than a formal garden. The same thing applies to your facial hair. Your body may not be a temple, but it is not a junkyard either. There is a faction of heavyset men who will use the excuse "I'm a Bear" to justify overeating or trying to put on the pounds. Big Bears are big guys naturally, and although "Beardom" is an attitude, not a body type, trying to bulk up is not the way to improve your Bear status. There is a line that is crossed when you realize you are no longer a Bear, but graduated to Girth and Mirth.

Miss UrsaKitt says:

"Get to the Bear Hug or Bath House party early... they have a limited number of large towels. And using two towels together makes you look a little hippy."

Bearobics

A Guide to Simple Workouts for the Bear Man

Just like the Freshman "10," there is the Bear "40." Once a man realizes he is a Bear he will gain an easy 40 pounds in less than a year. And he will spend the rest of his life wanting to lose it... some day.

The 501 Squeeze A warm up before working out is a good idea. Trying to fit into an old pair of jeans will get the blood pumping.

The Elbow Bend Using a 16 oz. can, the elbow bend can strengthen stamina. The can should touch the lips and empty. It is necessary to reload as weight diminishes.

Running Bar Laps Start first by pivoting the head to survey the track. Determine the most interesting route, turn and walk around the bar. Be aware that there will be men trying to stop you during your routine; remember: **This Time Is For You**. Do not stop until you achieve your goal. Also, this exercise can be coupled with the Elbow Bend.

The Singles Bicep Workout This excellent aerobic exercise is both fun and complete. Starting slow and building momentum, the work-out should complete itself with an appropriate cool down. A shower afterwards may be needed. Also, this is a popular group exercise, although only at specific Bally's in the Southeast.

The Beard
The Battle between Good and Evil

It has been said to be the hallmark of the Bear Man. A man without facial hair cannot truly be a member of the ursine clan. He can have a moustache and be called a Behr but to be a BEAR he needs a BEARD. Beards come in all shapes, sizes, colors, textures and thickness. It is significant that you pick the suitable beard that is correct for your face and conveys the message you wish to send. That message is on a sliding scale from Evil to Good.

The Goatee Family

Mostly associated with Satan, the sparseness of these styles often leads people to think the worst of the wearer.

The Beard Family

The extension of the sideburns to meet the hair on the chin leads to a softer more approachable look.

The Chin Puff is seen on anyone who can't grow a proper beard. Popular with the Beat generation, it is making a comeback on lead singers of SKA bands. Also known as a Soul Patch.

The Anchor is the most dramatic of these designs. Works with a pencil thin John Waters moustache. Note that it is an arrow pointing down toward the wearer's crotch or to Hell.

The True Goatee is an expansion of the Chin Puff where the hair never grows on the underside of the chin but only on the vertical face, like a mask.

A beard has always been a sign of virility and manhood, and thus is the main draw for anyone who is attracted to the male of the species. There are several reasons why a man grows a beard. It could be that he wants to assert his masculinity, it could be that he is too lazy to shave, or it could be that he is scared of razors as a result of being traumatized by seeing *Sweeny Todd* at an early age. A beard is the pride of being a man and grooming habits should be maintained. Haplessly rushing through trimming and stylizing only leads to an unmanageable muzzle. Take time to shampoo, rinse and repeat. And use a conditioner. Beard hair is wiry and needs to be controlled. It is not unlike that which grows in the pubic region. That is why these areas so easily mingle together.

The Balboa Goatee lets the hair grow and fully encases the chin. This sort of facial hair is best suited for those whose beard grows in thick and can grow in the shade out of the light of God.

The Hollywoodian is the first example of the goatee working with other facial hair. It does not mingle with the sideburns but instead connects to the moustache. This is the island of hair that circles the mouth, thus often looking like the evil vagina.

The Van Dyke is the most sculpted of these. As seen here it has ties to the Anchor pointing downward, but the attachment to the top of the head saves it from damnation. If Mary Magdalene could grow a beard, it would be this one.

The Classic Short Box is the most common of beards. Neatly groomed and trimmed, it is welcome in any Southern Baptist Church. It has a tendency to get disheveled when rimming.

The Chin Curtain is popular with the Amish and Mennonites.

The Jesus or **ZZ TOP** is the most natural of beards. It flows from the face and is grown the way God intended it to be. Payasses are optional for Hasidic Jews as are the fuzzy guitars.

The Beard as Woman

A "beard" in straight society slang is the word for that woman who is romantically linked to a man to conceal or cover up his homosexuality.

Famous Beards in History

Elsa Lanchester
Vivian Leigh
Liza Minnelli
Sylvia Fine
Phyllis Gates
Arianna Huffington

Body Hair Patterns
Shag, Wall to Wall and Berber

Chest Hair Patterns

The Canvas— this body is virtually hairless, allowing its lover to paint or draw on any hair that is missing. If there is hair present it is mostly on the legs and very fine. This body usually belongs to the Bear that has invested in tattoos.

The Nest— Placed nicely on the chest, this clump of hair is deceiving. When the owner wears a shirt open to the 3rd button, the Nest has the illusion of expanding all over the chest. It rarely reaches the nipple region. The clump, however, is often thick and full enough to run your fingers through.

The Dusting— Reserved mostly for Redheads and Blondes, the Dusting actually does cover most of the pectorals and maybe onto the belly, however not densely. Men who are "dusted" often have good tans.

The Love Trail— Starting at the nipples, all the hair on the chest and belly focus in one direction: toward the penis. This pattern can be found mostly on men with dark fine straight hair. A mini version of the trail, which extends from the pubic region to the belly button, is commonly found on Cubs and Mediterranean women. Also called **The Crab Ladder** for obvious reasons.

The Owl— This pattern is so named because it likens itself to a silhouette of a Horned Owl. The horns start at the shoulders and scoop down the neck-

line of the Bear. The pattern expands around the nipples, forming the head and then bulging out into the owl body on the Bear's tummy. The silhouette does not clearly cut off but fades into the sides of the Bear.

The Pelt— This Bear has hair everywhere and there are no set patterns or bald spots. The covering is evenly distributed around the entire body. The hair is usually a coarse curly hair that makes up the "Pelt" but falls out regularly. This Bear often has a clogged tub drain.

The Vicuna— This is the most covering you can get on one man. Named after the sweater, the Vicuna man is often thought to have on clothing when naked. Oddly enough, the hair on his head is rapidly disappearing. He will have male pattern baldness. This Bear also has the rear version of the Love Trail to his ass.

Hypertrichosis the medical term used for excessive body hair. Linked to genetics and mostly tying us to our evolution from apes, it can be as simple as thick hair on a man's chest or in some cases hair on the eyelids. The latter is a rare condition but it has occurred throughout history to monarchs and common man alike. Sadly enough, most people afflicted with this disorder are relegated to Sideshows, billed as the Wolf Man.

Body Hair Specialties

Paw Prints— Hair on the back that marks where the paws are placed in a Bear hug. These large patches of hair are approximately located evenly over the lungs and kidneys.

The Satyr— Associated with the mythological Goat Boy, this is the phenomenon of being hairy only below the waist. This is sometimes a stage of development for cubs in their late teens or early twenties. The mini love trail is present.

The Cum Shot— Usually due to a vitamin deficiency, an albino patch of white or gray hair will appear on the body. Sometimes on the head, like Lily Munster, this shock of no color is often found on chest or pubic area. This is not due to age where gray is sprinkled in but a distinct mark that has sex appeal. The owner is often called "Skunk."

The Tuft— The Tuft is a good indicator as to the hairiness of the Bear and is often thought to be the sexiest of body hair attributes. This bushel of hair is that which extends up and over the collar of a crew neck tee shirt leaving much to the imagination. The Tuft does not melt into the Beard. There is a definite line of neck skin that is visible. Also note that the Back Tuft exists, but is rare. Anyone with that much hair often does not wear a shirt, thus not allowing the Tuft to exist.

Other Hairy Beasts

Dogs

Man's best friend seems like the ideal pet for Bears. The friendliness of a Golden Retriever, the hairiness of a Sheepdog, the gruff façade of a Rottweiler, the bulkiness of a Bulldog; all equal Bear qualities. And yet the Bears that have dogs at all have small dogs: Pugs and Pekingese, Shih-Tzus and Yorkies, Dachshunds and Chihuahuas can be found in Bear households more often than the big dogs. Bears and dogs do go well together, as evidenced by the abundance of ursine attendees and trainers at the Westminster Dog Show, however dogs come in second to cats as the pet of choice.

Cats

Possibly due to their low maintenance and independence, cats are the most popular pets for Bears. For what other animal can someone just fill up the auto-feeder and auto-waterer, and clean the cat box before heading off to the next Bear weekend without worrying if Felix will be ok when you're gone? Truth is, the cat will be looking forward to your next Bear event so it will once again be Queen of the household. While it may seem contrary to the butchness of Bears to own a cat instead of a dog, Bears at least tend to own the less queeny breeds. Rarely will you see a Persian, Burmese or a Himalayan. They're too girly and pink. Bears are more apt to have tomcats, Maine Coons, and Russian Blues.

Bear Cat's Names
Urban Bear:
Miss Desmond
Suburban Bear:
BooBoo Kitty
Rural Bear:
Butch
Gen X Bear:
Josie
(of Pussy Cat fame)

Adornments to the Bear Body

Tattooing

The biggest problem for a Bear with a tattoo is shaving to have it done and shaving to show it off. A Bear with ink under his skin has to realize that there is most likely a layer of hair on top of it. The upper biceps and above the nipple on the chest plate are both areas prone to hair and, unfortunately, a great place for a tattoo. On the upside, hidden tattoos can mesmerize someone's gaze from across the bar. It evokes interest from an admirer and forces him to look deeply at the design to decipher it. He is trapped; hypnotized by your markings. By the time he realizes that the grizzly buried beneath the mat of fur on your chest has a prevalent hard on, you have sized him up and decided if he will want waffles or pancakes for breakfast. Also, the tattoo works wonders as a conversation starter. Ask anybody with one how many times they've answered, "did it hurt?"

Piercing

The fashion statement that seeped from the underground and reared its steel head is body piercing. Bears have the same fetishes as any healthy queer, so it's common to see a piece of metal protruding from his flesh. The hairy chest of a Bear can be decorated by having his nipples pierced. The silver circle bedded in fur is often hidden, but tends to be the most popular piercing. Those Bears who do have a Prince Albert or a Guiche also tend to own a copy of "Sailor's Knots Made Easy" and a butt plug or two. In other words, rough trade. Tusks can be found on Bears but detract from the fur around the face.

Branding is not a Bear thing— ever smell burning hair?

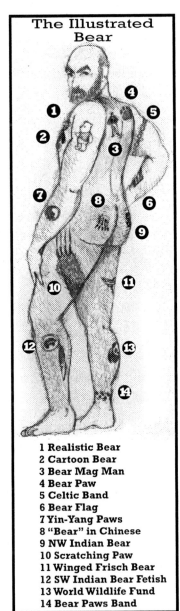

The Illustrated Bear

1 Realistic Bear
2 Cartoon Bear
3 Bear Mag Man
4 Bear Paw
5 Celtic Band
6 Bear Flag
7 Yin-Yang Paws
8 "Bear" in Chinese
9 NW Indian Bear
10 Scratching Paw
11 Winged Frisch Bear
12 SW Indian Bear Fetish
13 World Wildlife Fund
14 Bear Paws Band

Family Jewels

There are two schools of thought when it comes to wearing jewelry. First is that jewelry is not very masculine and therefore not very Bearish, so Bears do not wear jewelry. Or two, the Bear who does wear jewelry does so in the extreme by wearing at least five gold chains, one with an Italian horn, a few pinkie rings and a bracelet or two. In this case the amount of jewelry works because it balances out with the Bear's amount of body hair and his size. Jewelry that has found its way on to the bodies of bears are:

The Cockring

Mother always said, "Never wear jewelry below the waist," but Mother didn't have a penis and a scrotum. Cockrings enhance not only the orgasm but also the look of the genitals. The type of cockring is personal preference. The black rubber gasket type is common and recommended, as it does not catch pubic hair like rubber bands or the snap-on kind and it is inexpensive, so it is not upsetting when left in a trick's shower.

The Bear Run Pin

Not to be worn unless among a collection of other run pins. One pin looks awfully lonely all by itself and needs at least four other pins to make it work. Most times worn on the breast of a black leather vest with an AIDS ribbon and other small enamel pins. These pins will range from the inaugural pin given away at the opening of a new roller coaster to a pin commemorating IHOP's one millionth pancake.

The Bear Fetish

Usually seen as a pendant, this Indian bear shape is sometimes made out of soapstone, jade, silver, turquoise or plastic. The talisman is able to be purchased at many roadside attractions along Route 66.

The Living and Unwanted Adornment

Whereas most furry beasts in the forest will be infested with blood sucking fleas, Bears often encounter a different parasite: crab lice. Easily transferred from one crotch to the other, the little silvery white demons find a happy home in which to lay their eggs in the hair of a Bear's pubic area. "Crabs," as they are often referred to, are the silent pets of many a Bear, that cause itching and irritation.

They are preventable, as long as you look into your partner's crotch for the little critters before you start grinding your groins together. And make sure you look everywhere he has hair. They could be hiding, and then, before you know it, you got them in your beard because you didn't check his asshole. Thankfully, they are treatable. Over-the-counter RID or KWELL take care of the bugs and their eggs. It is a good idea to have a supply on hand for use after a Bear weekend. Depending on your amount of body hair, you may need a case.

"What is that in your mouth?"

A Bear's List of Substances

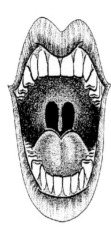

If the saying that goes, "you are what you eat," is true, then Bears would be a mixture of beer and pizza. What goes into the Bear body though is more than food; here we will examine what makes its way into the mouths (and other orifices) of Bears.

Hair— Bears have a tendency to end up with human hair doubling as dental floss, and swallowing over a lifetime an amount equal to a small raccoon. Of course it's not just the hair but what's on the hair that enters the body. If you are attacking a true Bear man, the only non-human substance in his hair will be basic soap– never a floral bouquet. Beware the Bear that smells like lavender. Also colognes are rare in the Bear community (and also aftershave, obviously), so the one piece of hair stuck on the back of your throat like a popcorn kernel is what is making you gag.

Man Sweat— Playing hard means sweating hard. Sweat glands on a Bear activate either in the heat of passion or if it's too damned hot outside. Although fur is said to be an insulator to keep coolness in, it still is like having on a fur coat when a furry man is on top of you. But once the sweat gets pouring, licking it can be an intoxicator. Slurping up the droplets in a Bear's armpit or butt crack is sweet even though it can be salty. Remember, food oils come though the sweat pores too, so if you and your date ate spaghetti for dinner, you will be sucking up some of his body-fermented garlic wine.

Proventil— Because a great many Bears suffer from asthma, the drugs taken for it should be mentioned. When Bears were cubs, they most likely were not the thin geeky nerd that was the last picked for indoor hockey who has asthma, but somewhere between high school gym class and going to the Bear bar, Bears develop the bronchial condition. It is not fatal, unless you get to The Dugout and realize your Proventil is back on the dresser. Doing a hit of asthma medicine is always good in a bar: it allows people to see that smoking near you might not be pleasant. You can always pull it out if the guy who's cruising you is not your type (you can also feign an attack), and anyone standing near you thinks you're doing some designer version of butyl nitrate.

Rogaine— It stands to reason that in a group of men where hair is important, a hair restorer should be on this list. Minoxidil, the active ingredient in Rogaine, in pill form, is a treatment for high blood pressure. Researchers crushed the pill and applied the solution to the scalp. Rogaine should not lower blood pressure since it is only applied topically to the affected area. The FDA approved a much stronger version of this miracle hair restorer (2% to 5%). It has been recommended only for men, not for women, as the side effect is growing facial hair. Attention Cubs — get that 5% via prescription for that full beard! On the other hand, Propecia, another miracle hair restorer, has sexual side effects and causes a "specific type of birth defect" if a crushed pill is handled by pregnant women. This cannot be a good thing.

Viagra— Although cubs may not need it, there are those Polar Bears that do. BEWARE: Viagra should not be used with Poppers!

Lube— Inevitably it will end up in your mouth, even though it was never intended to. Most lubricants have no real taste, they just leave a nasty coating on the tongue and teeth. The flavored ones that are intended for consumption still leave the coating. They just smell like the fake fruit markers made by Flair in the 70's.

And what's that up your nose?

Most likely it is an airhose that's attached to an **O₂** tank. It is not uncommon for Bears to suffer from Sleep Apnea or Idiopathic Hyposomnia. This bedtime disorder causes erratic breathing when sleeping. In other words, snoring, and usually loudly. Bears that suffer this disorder are prone to be forced out of a shared hotel room by his bunk mates. But sleep apnea is more than just making loud guttural snorts. It really is dangerous as it causes whoever has it to stop breathing which can lead to death. To combat the disorder some people sleep with oxygen being pumped into their nose through a tube. Others undergo a procedure where they have their throat scraped. That means at least six weeks of no deep throating. Therefore Bears will opt for a tube up their nostrils.

Poppers— The proper name is *AMYL NITRATE* if it's the ampule that's snapped or *BUTYL NITRATE* if it's the kind in the little brown bottle. They are classified as a hallucinogen, are synthetically created and legal. However, they're sold as video head cleaner or room deodorizers. The big deal with them is that they intensify orgasm and relax the muscles in your sphincter so you can take that well hung lumberjack who only tops. The perception of time is altered and slows down, but the rush doesn't last long (neither did the lumberjack). Too many hits at one time can cause the nasal passages to get inflamed and a head rush that leaves a bad headache. There are a whole slew of overdose symptoms ranging from nausea to decreased blood pressure and even death, but there are no withdrawal effects, so at least you never have to wear a patch to get unaddicted (a patch on hair is murder).

The Bear Body Dressed

It has been said that clothes make the man. They also make the Bear. The proper attire is as important as the beard. And more so when you consider that the wearer has total control over his wardrobe. He may not be able to grow a proper goatee, but he better own at least two flannel shirts if he is to think of himself as ursine. The Bear man is not a fashion victim, however, falling for current trends. His uniform is a mixture of comfortable machismo and easy access with a dash of Pugsley Addams. There are certain fabrics he should avoid, like velour and mesh; fads he should not follow, like droopy club kid pants and Sans-a-Belt, and designers he should not even consider like Versace (Baroque prints on silk never work with body hair, no matter how Italian you are). The rules for Bear dressing are not hard to follow. That, along with the solidarity factor of recognizing each other in airports, is what has kept the Bear look popular since even before the Bear movement evolved into something substantial.

1. Keep it simple. The lack of embellishment helps in keeping the look classic. Don't invest in an outfit that can only be worn once.
2. Keep it clean, although wrinkles are ok.
3. Make sure it's quality. Bears wear clothes hard, so invest in garments that are going to last.
4. Make sure it fits. You're big, buy big clothes, not so much for looks but for comfort. Too tight shorts can lead to wedgies and chafing.

The Flannel Shirt

The Flannel Shirt is a staple in any Bear's closet. Most Bears have at least three: One that is broken in but as intact as the day it was bought from L.L. Bean; One from Wal-Mart's Big Men's department that has the sleeves torn off at the shoulder and maybe a little frayed around the edges; One that can barely be called a shirt. It's been worn when washing the Jeep, cutting the grass, in the backroom of the Phoenix and it's stolen from your lover's side of the closet. It doesn't matter what color the flannel shirt is as long as it's plaid. The classic plaid flannel finds its heritage in the tartans of Scotland and on the backs of the Woodsmen of the Northwest— both very manly. Red and white, red and blue or blue and white plaids tend to be the most frequently seen on Bears. Only the bravest Bear will try pulling off pastel plaids. Buffalo Plaid, the wide black and red squares, works best on a larger body and Blackwatch Plaid is sporty and often found on shirts other than flannel.

TOPS

They seem to grow in your closet. One day you look and you have way too many tee-shirts and you don't wear most of them. Some because they just don't fit anymore, others because Fido Dido just ain't as cool as he once was.

1 The Black Tee - It will be from a Bear event and the neckline will be stretched out.

2 The Bar Tee - This one will be bought on vacation and worn in the local bar to show off where you've traveled.

3 The Naked Man Tee - It might be Dade Ursus or Tom of Finland. Either way you'll slip up one day and wear it to Wal-Mart.

4 The Bear Event Tee - For every event you attend expect a tee shirt with the local club's logo on it. Tee shirts from events earlier in the Bear movement usually came in black or white and suffered from Bad Art Syndrome.

5 The Hawaiian Shirt - Not part of the tee shirt family but manages to fit in with them. The Party Shirt. The louder the print the better. Never tucked in and always one button missing.

6 The White Tee With the Stain - Every shirt will have some sort of food that splattered on the belly, but the All White Tee Shirt will have tomato sauce or a mustard stain from the loaded hot dog outside Home Depot.

7 The Character Tee - Winnie the Pooh, Yogi Bear or That Grrrrl.

8 The Jersey - Any sport shirt will do but the football jersey looks best. The number will mean something.

Miss UrsaKitt says:

"Spandex, although a fun fabric for the bedroom, should never be worn, not even by Kate Moss"

BOTTOMS

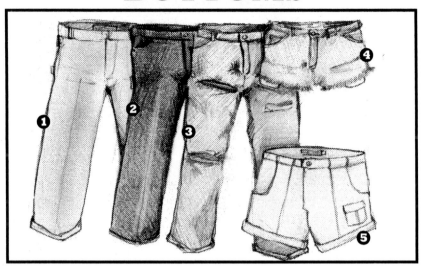

1 Dickies
Will be worn to a formal event because the Dockers were a tad tight. May have a small hole in the crotch.

2 The Old Levis
One size too small. They may be in black and bought for line dancing.

3 The Sluts
Ripped in easy-access areas. Sandpaper has been used.

4 The Obscene Cut Offs
The pockets will be hanging lower than the shorts.

5 The Hiking Shorts
Makes the legs look good.

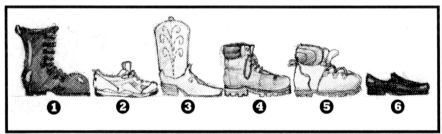

1 Military Boots
Doc Martens will also do. Shined at the Boot Black during leather night while you smoked a cigar acting real butch.

2 Reebok Cross Trainer
comes in wide with arch support.

3 Cowboy Boots
Highest heel a Bear will own.

4 Construction Boot
Never worn to a construction site and needs to be removed when in a sling to fit through the stirrup rings.

5 Mountain Hiking Boot
Highest elevation worn—the picnic at Pickle Gulch during OctoBearFest.

6 Loafer (optional)
Worn for the job interview at Microsoft and has never been polished.

VERSATILES

1 Hankie
Any color is acceptable
2 The Cowboy Hat
Black felt for winter, Straw for summer
3 The Baseball Cap
Liquor or Hardware brands are acceptable but the Bear cap is a must
4 Cock Ring
Rubber, Steel or Leather as long as it's washable
5 The Leather Cap
Either the Confederate style or a baseball cap is preferred. Avoid a leather jeff
6 Sunglasses
Silver mirrored and left over from the leather boy days. Increasingly difficult to find
7 Glasses
Wire frame are totally acceptable at the bar

8 The Union Suit
Worn for sex, not warmth. Be sure to clean after use. Wash alone, the dye will run.
9 The Leather Jacket
Black only, please and zippers only on slash pockets
10 Winnie the Pooh Underwear
For the underwear or underbear party
11 Armband
Should only be worn if you have a bicep. Cinched fat looks bad.
12 Plaid Boxers
Even a brief man must own one pair
13 The Leather Vest
With Bear run buttons and red ribbon
14 Dogtags
Not worn every day. Only for special occasions
15 The Chained Wallet
Leather Flag or Harley logo is optional

Where to Shop

Lane Bryant does not carry flannel shirts. Therefore it is important for Bear men to find shops that carry XXL sizes and cater to the Bear look. Most often, though, a store that sells lumberjack stuff will carry larger than petite sizes. With the sizing-up of American waistlines, it has become easier than in the past to find the right size, however you need to find the right clothes. Remember that old-man Cuban Guyabara shirts come in your size but you should never be seen in one.

Big & Tall Casual Male. The store

has nothing smaller than a 38 waistline. Good for businesswear but the sportswear is lacking. High percentage of Ban-Lon and gabardine but the place has been known to cruise and the salesmen are also portly.

Army Navy Stores. Never underestimate surplus stores for a good deal on manly duds. Camo prints and U.S.M.C.

tee shirts that are perfect for next month's military theme party. They also carry the whole rainbow of hankies and most likely the guy behind the counter can tell you what they stand for.

Bear Event Vendor Mart. Of course, the bigger the event, the bigger the mart. Some Bears have been known to stockpile a year's worth of clothing in one trip to the vendor mart at Bear Pride. Lots of caps, tee shirts and jewelry all sporting some sort of bear motif. The more unique ones sell out quick, so shop early. There is usually a stained glass vendor too.

Specialty Stores

Mr. S, *San Francisco*. Collars, cuffs, tit clamps and all your black clothing needs. Even the animal dildos are extra large.

REI, *Seattle*. Sporting Goods. The store itself is a Bear event. They brought the outdoors indoors. You won't see many Bears climbing the rock wall because they're cruising in the camping goods area. Plenty of Gore-Tex.

The Bear Store, *San Francisco.* Brush Creek Media Goods. Frish shirts, Bear Mag Logo merchandise, porn and bumper stickers. Think of it as the Bear's General Store.

The Giggling Grizzly, *Hot Springs CO.* A lot of tee shirts and sweatshirts with bears on them. Some of them are fierce and growling and some of them are cute and cuddly, but none of them are the two-legged kind showing their genitalia. The stuffed bear out front is posed for photo opportunities.

The Drag Queen and Leather Drag

Leather Boys and Drag Queens have a love/hate relationship. They have too much in common and don't want to admit it. Both camps are at the polar ends of gay culture, one being as butch and manly as possible, and the other trying to squeeze into a Bob Mackie knock-off. They both strive for sashes, however, and love to be the center of attention. Bears don't. Most Bears feel comfortable blending into the background wearing clothes that are not too conspicuous. This is not to say that Bears haven't been seen in chaps with a hairy butt hanging out. In fact, some Bears have one paw in the Bear community and another with the leather boys, but rarely will you find a Bear dolled up in a cocktail dress. So when a Bear does want to don big hoop earrings, it's usually in fun. Like straights at Mardi Gras in New Orleans or the Mummers Parade in Philadelphia, big burly guys are in drag because it's an event. Often you'll find bearded cheeks with rouge on them at queer events like Wigstock in New York, Southern Decadence in New Orleans or Fantasy Fest in Key West. Let the gender fucking begin!

Bear Quiz 2
Can You Draw the Proper Beard
on Garth Brooks?

Problem: Garth is in a quandary. He's performing at the American Music Awards in two weeks. He's hosting Saturday Night Live this week. He's also shooting a video between the two. He doesn't know what kind of facial hair would be the most appropriate. Can you draw the beard that would be most befitting for all occasions?

Solution: Anything would be fine for the award show as your appearance there is nebulous— just look at Aerosmith. For the video, Garth should have a goatee, because that is the sexiest on him and sex sells CDs. He won't have time to grow it in though because on SNL he is apt to do drag and should be smooth for that. So, for the video he'll have to glue on a fake goatee with waterproof glue, as the video is apt to have him in the rain. Therefore, the answer is no facial hair this week and start letting it grow next week.

CHAPTER THREE
THE BEAR'S HABITAT

where the breed dwells
or
"Where to go between closing time
and Happy Hour"

PART 1
CYBERSPACE

An Introduction to Cyber Habitat

The introduction to the wonderful world that exists in computers came to most Bears at a young age. There was a Christmas morning that a young cub woke up and opened his first Pong, Atari (or Sears knockoff) or Sega Video Game system. Or there was an afternoon spent at an arcade pumping quarters into Tempest, Centipede, or Space Invaders. (Little realizing this would be training for pumping quarters into a private video booth) Or there was computer camp that spent July out of the hot sun and in an air-conditioned room with a really cute counselor named Nick. The Bear recognized the computer as a tool and a toy. He became adept and built a career in spreadsheets, desktop publishing, or Quicken. He relaxed by finding the correct sequence of musical notes to take him to one of the many worlds of Riven. And while he was working and playing, he learned how to use the modem.

Cyberspace, The Last Frontier, came right into his bedroom. Given that a Bear is a Man and Men are traditionally the hunters in the tribe, Bears tend to look for things. Curiosity leads them to new realms. They become explorers. They become hunters. And what are they hunting? Of course, other Bears. In other words, Bears use Cyberspace as the world's always-open cruise bar and bathhouse.

The Three Parts of Cruising Cyberspace

Living in Cyberspace means entering a New World. It means you can create a new identity. It also means meeting new people. It means being frustrated that you only have a 28.8 modem because you don't want to spend the hundred bucks for a cable line and the nude photos of Rip Torn with a beard are taking forever! But it also means adventure without leaving your house. Most Bears know enough about cyberspace to get them into trouble, but trouble is what most bears are hunting for. In order for the hunt to be successful a Bear must master three areas:

Navigation
Knowing the layout of the web is clutch if you plan on cruising it. Although your objective will be different each time you approach this maze, you need to know how to find what it is you are looking for. Very often your first time on-line will result in a successful meeting with both you and your trick drenched in sweat, but you cannot rely on beginners luck very long. Learning how to get from point A to his crotch is valuable knowledge.

Information
Once you learn to navigate this Information Super Highway, you can find out most anything on the web. But realize this; While you may be looking for someone, someone may be looking for you. You are not just the tracker. You are also the prey and you may want to be caught. As both hunter and hunted you possess the unique knowledge of what information will work successfully as bait in the bear trap. So in traveling from point A to his crotch, you should be able to tell if it is a crotch you want to go to in the first place, or if it is a colossal waste of time.

Communication
The last step before actually meeting face to face for the conquest is relating to other men on-line. This could be done on electronic bulletin boards and email but very often connections are made in real time, due mostly because when you're hunting for sex, you want it now! This means once you have found his crotch, and determined it is a crotch you want to visit, if he is available at the present time there is no reason not to grab the opportunity and haul your cookies over to his joint for some unabashed fun. Mind you the Internet is world-wide, so you may need your passport in the haul of your cookies! Still learning to interact with one another on-line with grace, decorum and proper grammar is an ongoing process. Conversations on-line are often broken down to the most basic "noun-verb" sentences, but this is to be expected when typing is done mostly with one hand.

Navigation - **The Old Bear Network**

For the most part, no matter what you start out looking for or which way you head you will always seem to end up looking at nude photos.

START

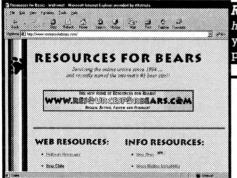

Resources for Bears
http://www.resourcesforbears.com
you can get to any number of personal web pages, bear sevices

Route 1 is good if your are traveling to a different location of the world. Start by going to **Web Resources, Bear Clubs**

Route 2
is good for surfing the web with no particular direction. This is often the more fun route. In **Web Resources, Bear Services** there are are a few good playful search tools

Bear Roulette
Sort of like the Mystery Date of the web- He could be a dream (ohhhh!) or a dud (awww!)

The Bear Quay
These Bears' personal web sites are rated - so he may be a dream or a dud, but if he rates 5 stars for his site, he's at least a good designer.

The Bear Ring
This could lead you to anything.

Bear Clubs Around the World

If you can't read a map without labels (like so many college freshmen), you can scroll down and find the clubs in alphabetical order by country.

Any Bear Club

Most bear clubs have a website. They will have info about the club and links to members' sites.

Any Bear's Personal Home Page.

This is one of the best features of the web. It's like looking into someone's psyche. One class in Psych. 101 will let you know who's husband material and who might be found atop a clock tower someday with a shotgun.

FINISH

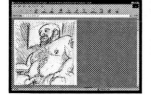

The Bear's Links

Most Bears will have a Gallery of Friends Page, photos of his trip to his last Bear event page and a photo page devoted to himself. From this last page you can get to his nude photos. These photos will be taken with a digital camera, so quality will be iffy. Other links include the Star Wars Web Site, Internet Movie Data Base, Nude Celebrity Photo Site.

Information - The 411

Gathering information is what the web is all about. With this tool you have access to find out almost anything. Just surfing around the Net, you could stumble across a site devoted to beards and facial hair or you could find out a high school classmate turned out to be the president of a Bear club in another part of the country. But what you turn up today may not be there tomorrow. The web changes quickly, so with that, any web sites mentioned in this book may or may not be there.

For Bears, the web has a lot to offer. There are plenty of men out there with home pages and hairy chests. Any search engine will bring up Bear-type men if you search "bear," but it will also bring up Teddy Bears, sports teams, real bears, and variations on the word "bear" (e.g. bearded collie, ball bearings, James Beard and Aubrey Beardsley). A thesaurus is a handy way to expand your search and use different words to search your interests. You'll also develop your vocabulary.

When searching, remember what you are looking for and your objective: hot steamy Bear sex. But somewhere along the way you may want to learn about more than how to insert a thermos in your rectum. The web also offers sites dedicated to variations on the Bear theme. For example; www.marthastewart.com.

Key Places to Get Good Dirt

Resources for Bears
www.resourcesforbears.com
This is the mother of all Bear sites. Kept immaculately up to date with all sorts of information, this is often the launch point for all Bears searching the web.

GayBC Radio
www.gaybc.com/bear.html
Talk is cheap: You can cyber away many an hour reading over lots of wordy websites, however if you want to listen to the Bear community, check out GayBC Radio's talk show, Bear In Mind. There is a backlog of interviews with members of the Bear community to download and a live broadcast.

The AOL Profile
Unlike the classifieds you find in the local fag rag, profiles on AOL can be more succinct and to the point, however, like them you must read between the lines. Most of the time the profile will be honest. Remember, this is a free thing you get with AOL. It's not a paid for ad in the paper that's looking for something, so you can believe most of what you read. Sorta.

Profile vs. Reality

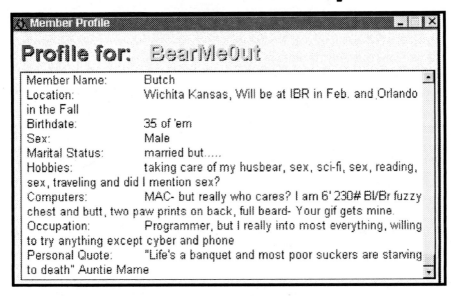

Member Profile

Profile for: BearMe0ut

Member Name:	Butch
Location:	Wichita Kansas, Will be at IBR in Feb. and Orlando in the Fall
Birthdate:	35 of 'em
Sex:	Male
Marital Status:	married but.....
Hobbies:	taking care of my husbear, sex, sci-fi, sex, reading, sex, traveling and did I mention sex?
Computers:	MAC- but really who cares? I am 6' 230# Bl/Br fuzzy chest and butt, two paw prints on back, full beard- Your gif gets mine.
Occupation:	Programmer, but I really into most everything, willing to try anything except cyber and phone
Personal Quote:	"Life's a banquet and most poor suckers are starving to death" Auntie Mame

REALITY BearMe0ut: this will be a clever derivative of the word "Bear."

MEMBER NAME: Butch is still a nickname (and usually reserved for the biggest Mary!). A real name will usually be presented, if asked. Beware of a last name— he's looking for something.

LOCATION: Putting in towns other than home is good. He'll be brought up in searches for those places he's also looking for sex in.

BIRTHDATE: Probably true— Bears are not super age conscious. Beware of "30ish"— that's 40 at least.

SEX: Check this one although it seems obvious. If you did a search for 'Bears' you may get Sally, who's ten and collects teddy bears.

MARITAL STATUS: The 'but' means he fools around, maybe with or without his mate.

HOBBIES: He's a bottom, he watches Star Trek, reads porn, and is willing to travel to get laid. And he uses AOL to meet men to do it.

COMPUTERS: Anyone who answers this one truthfully may not be someone you want to get to know. Using it for physical description is common and usually true. The GIF part is the kicker— he has a G rated one to send out but is looking for an X rated one to whack off to.

OCCUPATION: Programmer means he's attached to the computer. The rest means he's really horny tonight and wants to get off, however his computer is by the window visible from the street, or he gets AOL at work, so no cyber. His lover is home, so no phone. And he didn't proofread.

PERSONAL QUOTE: WARNING! Avoid anyone with this quote. Yards of chiffon will fall from his mouth AND he's unoriginal. Look for someone with a PERSONAL quote, not one stolen from a movie.

The Bear Code Alphabet Soup Part 1

The Bear Code is a universally accepted way to identify a Bear man on-line even though it is more confusing than the directions to MYST.

Started by two Bears in a Wendy's (imagine! Bears in a fast food place—who'd a thought) and based on sar classification code, the Bear Code has become a significant communication tool for men to clearly and concisely describe themselves without a photo.

The most obvious characteristic of a Bear is understandably his facial fur. So, that is the most logical place to begin. Using a capital "B" to denote "BEAR," we have added a sub-class characterizing "beard type" which combines a Bear's beard's length, thickness, and overall "keptness," numbered from 0 to 9 and defined in the following way:

"B" designation to give an idea of WHAT the person would look like with a beard.

B0 Little/no beard, or incredibly sparse
Such a beard is the absolute minimum that could ever be classified as a beard. We're talking 5 o'clock shadow, here! And yes, we are of the opinion that the beardless can still find company among the ursine!

B1 VERY slight beard
This is the kind of beard that people have who want to have a beard, but can't grow one. Or someone who is constantly at the 1-week phase.

B2 Slight beard
A beard kept VERY short at all times, or thinned out.

B3 Thin beard
A beard in all respects but kept thin and short.

B4 Mostly full
A beard that is full except for a few notice-able bald spots, or kept trimmed.

B5 Full beard
A full beard not generally trimmed, though not generally bushy. May have a few bald spots on inspection. Usually full and roundish beards fall into this category.

B6 Very full
A full beard, not trimmed. May be slightly bushy but very full, thick, full beards (more so than B5's) are B6's. B6's beards also generally are higher up on the cheeks than B5's.

B7 Longish/bushy beards
A full beard or slightly thin beard with longish fur. This beard is not trimmed and does come away from the chin.

B8 Very long beards
These beards are usually very bushy and

haven't seen clippers for a very long time.

B9 Belt-buckle-grazing long beards. The prototype is ZZ Top. Need we say more?

Using this scheme, it shouldn't be hard to narrow a person down to within 1 sub-class, although occasionally people may fall between two classes, and then the end result is left up to the person classifying, or one may use a hybrid designation (for example: B7/4) for those who vary across time (in the given range they spend more time near the first number).

While beards can be an observable trait of Bears, there are other things that different people take into consideration as to "what makes up a Bear," and things that people like in their Bears. So, bearing that in mind (pun intended) there are other criteria that can/should optionally follow the "B" designation.

It is not necessary to have a "grade" for each of these traits! For each there is a "neutral" value, which basically describes someone who is "average" or "unknown" within that trait. These "neutral" values are given below, but would not be reported--- treat them as either "default" or "assumed."

f - "The FUR factor." **Some Bears are particularly hairy about the rest of their bodies, others INCREDIBLY furry, yet others though rightfully Bears, have little or no fur on their chests, arms, legs, back, butt, etc. So, one of the following may be added to better describe a Bear's fur:**

f++ WAY above average fur
f+ above average fur
f furry in a Bearish sense
(none) "neutral," avg. fur from a sample population of both Bears and non-Bears
f- below average fur
f-- WAY below average fur--"Nair-smooth to the max!"

t - "the TALLNESS factor," **To describe Bears that are tall or short for their frame.**

t++ a virtual giant Bear
t+ taller than average
t tall but not very tall
(none) average height
t- shorter than average
t-- a Bear of very small stature

w - "the WEIGHT factor." **For those who prefer their Bears more or less fluffy.**

w++ a round Bear/BIG TEDDY Bear
w+ a big boned Bear
w Bear with a tummy
(none) average weight for frame
w- a thin Bear (otters!)
w-- a bony Bear

c - "the CUB factor," **For the junior up and coming Bears.**

c++ complete daddy's boy
c+ definite cub
c cub tendencies
(none) not "cubbish"
c- looks like a cub but isn't

d - "the DADDY factor,"
For the cubs, etc.
d++ DADDY with a
vengeance (even his
parents call him SIR!)
d+ definite DADDY
d daddyish tendencies
(none) not a daddy
d- looks like a daddy
but isn't

Note there are now also
HYBRID classes "cd" and
"dc":
cd A cub with "daddy
tendencies"... Sort of
like a "grown up cub."
dc A daddy with cub-
like tendencies/features.
dc- More daddy than
cub
d+c REAL daddyish and
also VERY cubbish
(etc.)

g - "the GROPE factor":
This is the amount one
likes to be touched or
pawed etc.
g++ Love to
grope/paw/touch etc.
Will attack without
warning. Gives hugs to
hot otherwise unknown
Bears on the street in
open daylight.
g+ likes to be touched
most of the time
g Generally outgoing
with ursine affection, a
little more reserved
about place/person...
(none) Average amount

of receptivity to being
touched
g- Generally doesn't like
people to invade his
personal aura/lair.
g-- You touch my bod, I
break your face!

k - "the KINKY factor"...
for those who dare.
k++ likes just about
EVERYTHING... we mean
EVERYTHING!!!
k+ picks and chooses
according to likes; will-
ing to consider new
ideas
k open minded. Might
choose SOME things on
the "menu"
(none) kinky neutral
k- has definite
ABSOLUTE dislikes
k-- totally vanilla

s - "SEX (ok, SLUT) fac-
tor." In SOME people's
Bear codes, "s" might
really mean "k" (since
"k" WAS originally "s" in
the earlier versions...).
s-- strictly monogamous-
ly/relationship oriented.
No outside affairs, or in
some cases, sex ONLY in
relationships
s- relationship oriented.
Prefers a formal sort of
relationship over play-
ing around, however the
scope of the word rela-
tionship is not defined
here.

(none) relationship neu-
tral
s neutral wrt to relation-
ships/monogamy.
s+ will form relation-
ships which are general-
ly open-ended
s++ strictly polygamous,
prefers very open rela-
tionships ONLY.

m - "the MUSCLE fac-
tor"... for those who like
meat on them bones.
m++ Arnold
Schwarzenegger is that
you?
m+ definitely works out
or is a ranch hand
m some definition/blue
collar
(none) muscle neutral

e - "the ENDOWMENT
factor"... sometimes a
size queen's gotta do
what a size queen's gotta
do.
e++ gets complete
respect even from
straight men
e+ gets attention
e noteworthy
(none) endowment neu-
tral

h - "the BEHR factor"...
for behrs (men without
beards but Bears). You
might also put a paren-
thesized number for the
"B" designation to give
an idea of what the per-

son would look like with a beard.
h behr (moustache no Beard)
h+ Definite BEHR (moustache no Beard)
h- no Beard OR moustache! (very rare but still cave dwelling)

r - "the RUGGED/OUTDOOR factor."
r++ "Grizzly Adams"
r+ Flannel/jeans/C&W really *are* second skin
r Spends some time outdoors/camping
(none) rugged neutral
r- prefers indoor-type activities (techie or 3-piece)
r-- never seen in the outdoors at all.

p - "the PECULIAR factor"
p Some idiosyncrasies — no judgement made to whether these are "good" or "not so good"

q - "the *Q* factor (ahem)"
q for Bears who are out —WAY out— and love every minute of it. Stereotypes be damned, break out the chiffon and everything else, because girlfriend, as

Auntie Mame says "Life is a banquet and most poor bastards are starving to death!" (For the stunned reading this — yes, Virginia, "q" is a GOOD thing just like "t-- and t++ are GOOD things", "w-- and w++ are GOOD things"; nothing negative should be associated with the *labels* pertaining to classification!)

ADDITIONAL PUNCTUATION
The following aren't graded, they are just flags attached to the overall classification:

v for variable, said trait is not very rigid, may change with time or with individual interaction (e.g., some guys who are generally REAL daddies, may turn into REAL cubs occasionally, etc.) ?
For traits where there is no HARD information available and the value is completely guessed at: e.g., a picture of a hot Bear that LOOKS like a rugged outdoorsman, r+? but in reality could be a 3-piece suit Bear. For traits which are observed but uncertain,

e.g., a guy who is wearing a lot of clothes, so you can't be SURE he's an f+, but his forearms REALLY suggest that he is, hence f+: For cases where the trait is as close to a prototype as possible, or an exemplary case of a specfic trait... e.g., the ultimate f++! For indicating "cross-overs" or ranges. A guy who goes from k to k++ depending on the situation (i.e., mostly "k") could use k(++) You can make the punctuation as detailed as desired, although the best ones to read are the ones which are the most clear and simple to understand.

NOTE: None of the classification materials in any way suggests a ranking or value judgement, in terms of what constitutes a "better" Bear. Every person has their own favorite type!

Communication
Where your message goes

Banging drums begat smoke signals that begat writing letters that begat the postal system that begat the pony express that begat telegraphs that begat telegrams that begat telephones that begat CB radios that begat computer communication that begat banging each other.

Your Message

Real Time Communication
Much like a visual C.B. Radio: People have handles and trucker types are looking for blowjobs. More than one conversation is going on at once. Misspellings are common due to typing with one hand.

Non Real Time Communication
You have the time to plan out your thoughts and express them in a coherent way. This will often lead to ranting and babbling on and on.

One on One Chat
Private chat, no one but you and your cyber buddy will see it, unless he has a group of friends around his terminal. Have your stats and photo ready for a fast response.

your message will result in another photo of a stranger whose name you'll forget

Buddy/Notify List
Otherwise known as The Chronics. These are people you see online a lot and avoid after awhile.

your messages will be playful but will lead to nothing because he lives in Denmark and he's become a sister and it would be weird

Chat Rooms
Group with like minded interests, usually sex or geographical location. Best way to improve your typing skills is by trying to keep up with the banter.

your message will be seen by the the entire room and only the wrong guys will respond

Email
Although faster than snail mail, the recipient still may not answer it right away. Use the subject line so your letter is not discarded with the spam.

your message will be seen by his lover who knows his password and responded to with every joke that's been forwarded to him

Bulletin Boards
Where most electronic communications started, this way is no longer the most popular way to get your message out. Still seen on websites as Guest Book.

your message will get lost because the BBS was closed

Mailing Lists
Depending on the topic this could be a daily or twice daily email. If you don't have friends who email, this is a way to ensure hearing "You've Got Mail" Best used for hooking up when traveling.

your message will be lauded by few quietly and disdained by many vocally

72

Servers
Alphabet Soup Part 2

To be on-line requires a server of some type and a modem, the device that lets your computer talk to other computers. Technology is constantly improving these devices and programs so both the modem and the server you have right now will be obsolete by the time you are finished reading this section of the book. The phone line to your computer will need to be replaced by cable to your TV and you will change your server each time you get a better rate.

AOL - America On Line
Often called AOHell, this server has parlayed itself into being the most popular on-line service provider, and mostly it has done it by making it so simple even morons can use it. It has colorful, easy-to-read graphics. It is not the oldest, it's just the one that marketed itself well enough so that almost everyone would be on AOL or at least know about it. This has been accomplished through mass mailings of CDs that make swell coasters.
Chat room: BEARS4BEARS: Limited number of people let in so it could be a wait, however as soon as you are in a chat room expect to be bombarded with spam offering "free hot teen pussy pics."

AOL IM
America On Line
Instant Messenger
It is an easy download and it's free. It is just your buddy list and the means to IM them. You can't go into chat rooms or have the other services of AOL, but after a few years, all you do is IM anyway.

IRC - Internet Relay Chat
Most people who are on IRC are graduates of AOL. Although America On Line is visually more pleasing and easier to use, the limitation on what is and is not appropriate on-line talk is not conducive to picking up other men for a quickie or for phone sex. IRC is just plain smuttier.
Chat room: From #gaypoppersex to #gayamputee, there is something for everyone. And that includes Bears. Most Bears hang out in one of the oldest rooms, #bearcave, but an alternative is #nekkidbears. An unlimited number of people fit in the room. Easy to send photos and files unless the recipient is on WebTV.

CUSeeMe, ICUII or Net Meeting
Once you have mastered talking and sending photos, you can move on to words with "sorta" real time photos. However, a jerky stream of images that comes very close to the SciFi promise of a picture phone, still looks like you're receiving a porn movie from the Mir Space Station. In ICUII make sure you start your "comment" with "bear." This will make it easier for grouping and sorting.

ICQ
One of the most Orwellian ways to communicate, ICQ erases identity by replacing your name with a number. And when using ICQ, as soon as you sign on to the Internet, anyone who has your number knows you're on. Big Brother is watching you and he knows where you're surfing.

Conversing On-Line - Standards and Practices

There are certain rules of communication to which polite society adheres in order to maintain a standard of gracious living. Those rules simply do not apply when on-line. The standard is in the extremes — either quite Neanderthal or exquisitely worded. There is very little middle ground. In order to meet and mate fast, quick short abrupt semi-sentences are traded until you find the one who will chat the cum out of you. Then typing can become as descriptive as a Harlequin Romance.

The Greeting
A simple hello to a stranger or a <<<POUNCE>>> can work for some-

one on your buddy list. Typing "stats?" or "photo?" is done but rather rude.

The Stats
Using the Bear Code is good, but if you don't have your decoder ring handy, it's tricky. Simple abbreviations work best. Remember: bl for blue and bk for black. Often br/bl is read as brown hair/blue eyes. Clearly the abbreviations state that this man's hair is blue.

The Photo
Make sure it's a good photo of you, with you looking at the camera. Quick Cam often makes men look like they are in a fish bowl and looking at the monitor while your shutter goes off makes you look goofy. Test the photo on a friend's machine. Send it to him

Chat Shorthand

:)	Smiley	((_!_))	Jiggly Ass	AFK	Away from Keyboard
:O-)	Bear smiley	("") ("")		LOL	Laugh out Loud
;)	Wink		Paws		
:O	Oh!	@--}-----		ROFL	Rolling On the Floor Laughing
:-{)	Man with a moustache		Rose		
[:)	Man with a flattop	ALL CAPS	Shouting	ROFLMAO	Rolling On the Floor Laughing My Ass Off
:^)>	Man with a goatee	((((handle))))	Shout Hello		
(I^)	Geordi La Forge	{{{{{ handle }}}}	Hug	IMO	In My Opinion
8=>	Dick	STATS Gifs	vital statistics	OMK	Over My Knee
8===>	Bigger Dick	jpegs		OMG	Oh My God
8==>.....		or tffs	images	BTW	By The Way
	Dick Shooting	(g)	Small grin	BRB	Be Right Back (also means "I have to dump")
(_!_)	Ass	(G)	Big grin		
(_*_)	Asshole	(EG)	Evil grin		
(_$_)	Tight Ass				

and ask how it looks. It may look great on your machine but you have your monitor set to a plethora of colors. Your best bet is a good clear black and white. Also resize it so it's quickly sent and received. Always send a G rated one first; the Bear on the receiving end may be underage or from the vice squad.

Chat or Banter

This is often the exchange of quips amongst cyber buddies that are not in the market for sex. Witty repartee will gain you respect in a chat room, and like the French court, ridicule will gar-

nish admiration from your cyber peers. However timing is everything. The more skilled at typing you are the better. If you have a great comeback but it took you too long to respond, just forget it. Typing it in late will look desperate and sad.

The Sign Off

Always say good-bye to those who you were chatting with, as you may want to chat with them again. Using the excuse "I was bumped" for your leaving abruptly will only work for so long. Sooner or later someone will tell you you need a new server.

The Conversation

Actively talking in the room is not necessary. All you need to do is look for a handle that you like and start an engaging conversation. Be warned, however, most conversations are monosyllabic. For example a conversation may go like this:

BearA: Hi
BearB: hey
BearA: how are you?
BearB: good - u?
BearA: fine
Then a pause for a while because BearB is finishing up a conversation with someone that's going nowhere- so he turns his attention back to BearA
BearB: stats?
BearA: 5'11" #255 balding but very hairy bearded - u?
BearB: WOOF!
***BearB is In Seattle 34 240 5'10" flattop full beard light dusting right nipple pierced.**
(BearB has been asked this before and has ready an instant reply)
BearA: woof
BearB: where?
BearA: Nashville
BearB: Kinda hard to get a bj that

far away **LOL**
BearA: coming to Spring Thaw this year
BearB: kewl - top/bottom
BearA: Top
BearB: :) -bottom here
BearA: cool- photo?
BearB: trade?
BearA: need to email - beara@bear.net
BearB: webtv?
BearA: yes

The conversation can go in a few different directions from here— either BearB will move on to someone else who has a real computer or the photos will be exchanged and they will hook up at Spring Thaw.

The exchange of information is riveting. And also void of most articles and pronouns. Obviously there is a code that needs to be learned in order to communicate on any real time chat. Mind you that both bears most likely have 4 or 5 other conversations going on at the same time so this sort of computer shorthand is almost a necessity.

The BML

Non Real Time communication involves posting messages and receiving them. To do this a Bear must have an email account. Once a Bear has an established email address he can receive electronic messages and images from many lands. He can also enjoy the wonders of junk email, or spam, and he can subscribe to bulletin boards, newsgroups and mailing lists. For the most part, bulletin boards and newsgroups grew during the early stages of Internet communication. It just so happens that a great many of them were and are sexual in nature. Mostly heterosexuals finding ways to get their rocks off, the budding gay community, also being sexual in nature, started making their presence known in this new form of meat market. Then in 1983 a Bear named Steve Dyer met a Bear named Brian Gollum during a computer-based gay issues-discussion group conference in San Francisco. Eventually one said to the other "Hey, we should have an electronic forum just for guys like us" and thus the Bears Mailing List was born in 1988. The birth was not as easy as stated here but to truly appreciate the scope of how the BML was created and formed, one must understand all the jargon and terminology that goes along with being a computer geek. But even those Bears that have only rudimentary computer skills and AOL as their on-line server still have the ability to participate in the banter that occurs on the BML.

The main thrust of the BML is to allow Bearmen and their admirers to post their opinions and observations of Bear life to an ongoing electronic memo that is emailed out to subscribers. Topics, or threads, are brought up for discussion and run their course over many issues of the BML. The potential of sharing information on the political platforms of various candidates to All-Star Wrestling or the medical advances in the treatment of STDs to the boxers vs. briefs debate is phenomenal. With a subscriber base that numbers in the tens of thousands and in countries as far away as Thailand, Russia and South Africa, Bears have a unique opportunity to be educated about foreign cultures and where the local Bear bar is when they are traveling abroad. The novice to the BML may be confused at first. Like a soap opera, the BML is a continuing saga with various conversations going on at once. But with his second issue, the novice will be right in the swing of things, typing out a rebuttal to someone's comment on "Bears that eat paté" or some other substantial topic. Although the BML is edited (a thankless job) submissions are rarely censored. The job of the editor is to cut off a thread if it gets too long or if the topic has strayed into the area of non-beardom. Therefore threads are usually relegated to eating, Bear events and sex (the latter two being almost the same topic).

Common Threads
cut or uncut
Richard Karn sightings
recent Bear event-
praise and bitch
introductions
"I'm visiting BFE...."
monogamy
sexy Bear celebrities
science fiction
beard grooming
flaming one another

Ways to Not Get Caught Cyber Cheating on Your Lover

Miss UrsaKitt says:

First and foremost, cheating is not good. You shouldn't do it. But your mother also told you not to stick strange things in your mouth and you do that. So if you must cheat, and you are in that odd Bear couple that is not open, cyber cheating is the safest way to do it. Here are a few tips to keep your playful cyber habits a secret, however your hubby could have also read this book.

Don't tell your lover your password for any account. If he gets into your email, that could be a disaster, but even worse is if he signs on as you into a chat room.

Delete all incriminating email. And make sure you empty the recycle bin. If the letters are too good and steamy to throw away or you want to keep them for blackmail reasons later, bury them good. Mark them with some technical name that your lover will avoid.

Feign indifference. Let him think that you think dirty talk on-line is funny, and not sexy. Let him look over your shoulder sometime while you both giggle your way through cyber sex with some clod in Saskatchewan who is really into it. Don't let the trick on the other end of the line know you're jerking him around. It's bad form, and as long as he's getting off, what he don't know won't hurt him. But with your hubby, as Evita says, "Better to win by admitting a sin than to lose with a halo." So he knows you do it, he just doesn't know you get into it.

Keep all photos sent to you in the same place and then put them on a zip disk at the end of your session.

Set up a fake AOL account that only you know exists.

Set up a Hotmail account. Then all mail will never be at any computer but on the web where you can only see it with a password. It's free and easy to use anywhere there is access to the web.

Use a Phone Card when making long distance sex calls so no odd numbers appear on the bill.

Clear the caller ID after you receive a call.

Block your phone number when calling with *67 so that your friend on the other end doesn't get your number and call back when your husband is home.

Or you could just invite your lover to join you in your cheating.

PART 2
the BEAR CAVE

The Habitat that has a Mortgage

The biggest statement of independence is to have a space you can call your own. A Bear's first apartment is how he will acquire this independence and freedom: freedom to leave porn all about, freedom to fart wherever he feels like it and freedom to decorate. NOTE: *decorate*, not *renovate*. This is the biggest problem with apartment living. If a Bear has a yen to move a wall or rip up the shag and install parquet, his landlord will frown on this. Therefore, when the urge to recreate his space can no longer be squelched, a Bear will buy a house.

Apartment Dwelling Some Bears spend their entire adult life paying rent. These men tend to be Urban Bears in big cities where owning a house is either cost prohibitive or simply just not done. The beauty of having an apartment is twofold. They are transitory: if the neighborhood you moved into 5 years ago all of a sudden attracts the wrong element (read: young couples with kids) then when your

lease is up you can move to the newest gay ghetto in town. The other plus is when something goes wrong, you can call maintenance. And maintenance men are notoriously big hairy types.

The House Once a Bear has a house, all those shows on HGTV make sense and become prime viewing. Inevitably the house will be in an "up and coming" neighborhood that has fallen into disrepair. As the cycle insists, queers will move into the area, renovate and thus, raise property values. The butch thing to do is open a Home Depot charge account, buy power tools and start customizing. The queer thing to do is subscribe to *Victoriana*, and anally recreate, down to the Arts and Crafts wall paper and tongue and groove wainscoting, a gingerbread Queen Anne cottage that is the showplace on the local "Tour of Homes."

Furnishing When it comes to the design and decorating of a Bear space, three rules apply: Comfort,

Hardware, Tool and Machine Companies That Have Logo Tee Shirts

Wolf

Husky

Stanley

Craftsman

Black & Decker

Skil

Rigid Tool

DeWalt

Bosch

Hilti

Makita

Milwaukee

Behr Paint

Caterpillar

Durability and Manliness. For these three reasons the most important thing to stay away from is wicker! In terms of comfort, a wicker chair cannot compete with a La-Z-Boy. Even on a patio, Adirondack wide board seats work better than woven reeds. And beware, wicker seats have been known to catch the hair on the back of the legs. (Think Epilady.) As for durability, wicker does hold up well. It's just the creaking that leads one to think the chair is breaking. When sitting down, a Bear wants as little noise as possible. And let's face it, Laurie Partridge is manlier than wicker. With the exception of Louis the Anything furniture, wicker is perhaps the most feminine of household goods. Other bad choices in this department are inflatable furniture and beanbag chairs. Both make your thighs sweat and it is hard to make a graceful exit out of them. Beanbags are good for sex however: easy to manipulate to any position and the vinyl makes for easy clean up.

Landscaping Once the inside is done, the exterior needs to be tended to. The best thing to do is to hire someone else for this. Preferably a Bear who works with his shirt off, glistens with sweat and needs a cool lemonade when the day is done.

Miss UrsaKitt says:

"When hiring a contractor, remember: A gay one will never question why you need a drain in the bedroom or need reinforced ceiling beams with good sturdy steel hooks"

The Bear's Den or Living Room

The Bear's Den is the hub of the house. Here is where entertaining is done (i.e.: when entertaining parents and not tricks). Arrangement of the furniture is important, leaving enough room for wide traffic flow.

The Kitchen

More than any other room in the home, the hearth is a favorite among Bears. Of course the bedroom is also a favorite, so it isn't amazing that Bears sometimes confuse the two. Cookie crumbs can be found in the rumpled sheets of a king-sized bed. There is always a half empty glass of something on the night stand and a half-full bag of Skittles next to the lube in the night stand drawer. And very often the meal most eaten in bed has a full beard and goes by the name Daniel.

In contrast to eating in the bedroom, the kitchen frequently offers the best

1 big oversized sturdy couch built well enough for two full grown men, complete with a handmade afghan crocheted by Grandma. Cat hair is also visible

2 tchotchke lamp from a garage sale— a gift from a Bear friend

3 La-Z-Boy— again, overstuffed and built for a workout

4 teddy bear collection: mostly gifts from straight relatives or from travels around the globe

5 the expensive collectible bear from the Steiff collection kept out of reach of visiting nephews

6 a spittoon filled with flowers— an idea stolen from *House Smart*

7 a beer stein from Berlin or the German Pavilion in Epcot

8 a bear fetish carved from stone: bought at a local art show

9 good framed photos of the family

10 CDs— *Patsy Cline's Greatest Hits*, anything by Garth Brooks or Brooks and Dunn, the Stephen Sondheim Collection, Reba McEntire Live, <u>The Adventures of Priscilla</u> soundtrack, Pet Shop Boys *Very*, Jimmy Somerville *The Singles Collection.*

11 videotapes— copies of *Home Improvement*, and *Iron Chef*, the PBS series on the Civil War, and *The Women* taped from A&E

12 framed posters: *La Cage aux Folles* and *Beauty and the Beast* or some city festival or skyline

13 the model of the Starship Enterprise bought at the last Trekker Convention

14 a big screen TV so Al is life-size

15 pizza boxes from last night or week

16 non-porn magazines— e.g., *Martha Stewart Living*

17 THE KITCHEN and the fridge— well stocked with Budweiser, Diet Coke and Healthy Choice Microwave French Bread Pizzas

18 MYST calendar

19 window boxes— a weekend project from Home Depot Classes

20 a bear footprint bought at Bear Pride the first year you went

21 poster of *Bears Dancing*— bought at the National Gallery during the Pride march. Well framed and matted in hunter green

22 A fireplace to snuggle in front of

---

opportunities for interludes usually reserved for the abode. The gadgets from Lechter's alone could make a participant in IML blush at the thought of all their alternative uses. As long as the table is sturdy enough, re-enacting scenes from *The Postman Always Rings Twice* can be fun. And then there is the food. A voracious appetite for food as well as sex is a common trait among Bears. Thus the combination of both seems ideal. However remember that even the most run-of-the-mill kitchen sex recipes like chocolate syrup and Redi Whip, are a mess when mixed with belly hair and still have just as many calories as if they were on top of a banana split.

The Hibernation Chamber

The Ursine Lair is the most versatile room in the home. Serving not only
as a place of rest, the bedroom must be able to mimic various other rooms
that may or may not be part of the house. Very often it is used as a game room,
sewing room or dining room and once in a while as a studio for
amateur video making (depending on the quality of the web cam).

The Teddy Bear Collection

Your First Teddy
Your mother saved it,
the fur is hard and the
nose is chewed off.

A Lot of Pooh Poohs don't come
single. Oh, you may start out with
one, but all of a sudden you have a
whole tribe of bears in red shirts.

The Ugly Bear Usually a
gift from a lover. It is too
ugly to be cute and he's
abnormally heavy.

1 hat rack

2 calendar of local firemen for charity

3 dirty flannel shirts that made it to hooks on the wall

4 the computer complete with MYST, AOL, IRC and a host of dirty picture downloads

5 empty or half-empty cans of diet soda

6 THE BATHROOM - tub drain is clogged with hair, toilet needs to be cleaned and the medicine cabinet has a Groomsman, a pair of scissors and a moustache comb. Shower curtain from the Laura Ashley Collection

7 BEAR XING sign stolen on a late night road trip

8 good high-tech stereo system— note hidden speakers

9 top drawer- socks; middle drawer- the Bear Party Videos and the current Porn Magazine; bottom drawer- the jeans that will fit again someday

10 Deadhead dancing bear sun catcher. It was a gift

11 window treatment from IKEA

12 throw rug from an Indian reservation bought on a cross country trek with your last lover

13 towel that hasn't made it to the hamper

14 a rough log king-size bed with bedding by Ralph Lauren

15 NIGHT STAND with photo of current lover, classic reading lamp and a top drawer with lube and condoms

16 a queeny ERTE print that was bought before you discovered Bear art (glass is cracked from last move)

17 a stuffed bear from the current lover

18 a Grizzly Adams lunchbox, picked up at a thrift store (paid too much for it, but couldn't resist Dan Haggerty)

19 photo album of renovations of house or trip to Seattle

20 Klingon mask from last Halloween

21 candles for a romantic night— pine scented

22 cross-stitch pillow from a distant aunt

23 small framed Tom of Finland drawing, a guilty pleasure

24 phone by the bed for calling the guys you just met on-line

25 the hidden toy box with all sorts of fun stuff

26 shoebox for work boots

27 folded flannel shirts on top of towels for after sex

Dress-up Bears These are bears with costume changes. Some are butch, some are regular Barbies with all the accessories.

Foreign Bears From your tour of Europe. You bought one in Munich and the widow you befriended got you the Paddington in London.

The Collectible It's the bear that comes with its own coffin. It's worth too much to even take out of the box and put on display.

The Garage as Playroom

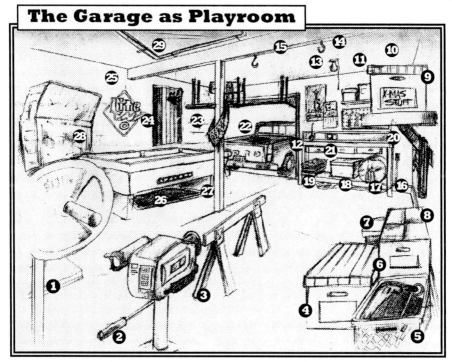

Cultivating a proper playroom can take time, effort and a great deal of money: Party toys ain't cheap. It also can involve a lot of cleaning products.

The Family Car

From the age of 16 all men have used the automobile as a tool for cruising. The car is an extension of a man's personality. The car is often said to be a phallic symbol. The car is a message to the world of a man's sexual prowess. Therefore a Bear's car must be rough, stylish and still offer enough room between the steering wheel and his belly so that his boyfriend's head has room to bob.

Like clothing, a car must fit. A Bear in a Miata is like a Bear in a Speedo; It may

be sexy in some aspects but it's just gonna be uncomfortable if you're in it for more than an hour. Along with Bears, the yuppies and rednecks have popularized what are deemed Bear-mobiles— Sport Utility Vehicles and Pick-up Trucks.

Both are truly American. Both are made for hauling camping gear or backdrops for Bear contest stages, both are masculine without being fueled by testosterone (like low-riders), and both offer large flat areas that allow for making out in a car (most back seats do not have enough room for two Bears to romp around like Rizzo and Kiniki).

1 workout bench that has been used for sex— grease stained
2 video camera— ready to go but battery is dead
3 sawhorse, as seen in at least one pictorial in every porn mag
4 box of gadgets created from the Home Cooking section of *Bear* magazine
5 old milk crate that holds the sling and chains
6 box full of old teddy bears from past lovers
7 the "industrial" toybox
8 cotton rope (never nylon) 15 yards worth
9 Christmas decorations, not including the crotchless Santa costume (it's in the attic and needs to be cleaned!)
10 leather scraps from trying to make your own harness
11 empty box to "straighten" up for when Mother is coming to visit
12 Steve Kelso Calendar stuck on July
13 local Bear bar or Dade Ursus

poster
14 light bulb....the black light is hidden in the industrial toy box
15 good sturdy hooks for the sling
16 electrical cord that can reach the whole garage
17 sleeping bag
18 camping gear
19 stack of old porn mags
20 drawer with lube, condoms, poppers and hardtack candies
21 oil can
22 the Pick-up
23 leather sash, a souvenir from that night with Mr. Bear 1995
24 the Bear Flag
25 neon beer sign
26 old Brunswick pool table from the now closed bowling alley
27 water resistant cover for the pool table
28 old mattress complete with stains
29 inconspicuous mirror on the ceiling, and it needs dusting

Whereas most SUVs and Pick-ups are manly, there are certain models that are gayer than others. Any SUV that has only two doors and a hatch, that is an automatic transmission, that is loaded with all the electronic gadgets, that comes in a "Grand" or "Luxury" edition, that has a sun roof, and that still touts that it is built for off roading is just like a gay Bear man. Pick-ups that are small are gay.

Appropriate Stickers

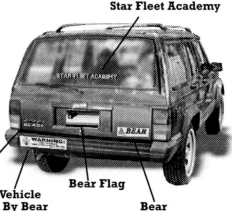

Star Fleet Academy

I Brake For Bears

Bear Flag

Warning: Vehicle Protected By Bear

Bear

Bear Quiz 3
Experts in the Field

Problem: *Jack has to make a decision. He has decided to follow a guru of better living and heed all of their advice, only he can't decide whom he should follow. Using the information in the grid, help Jack deduce the best expert for his life.*

	Bob Vila	Burt Wolf	Christopher Lowell	Martha Stewart
Show	*Home Again*	*A Taste for Travel*	*The Christopher Lowell Show*	*Living*
Network	A&E	Travel Channel	Discovery Channel	Lifetime
Point of the Show	Old home renovations	Eat your way around the world	Quick cheap decorating	Gracious living
Real Point of the Show	"We can make shit shine in a ghetto"	"Look at this incredible food and interesting people I meet"	"I'm trying to steal Lynette Jennings' audience"	"Live my way or be shunned by society"
Host is like...	Marlon Perkins "I'll wait here while Jim goes down the river to wrestle that alligator"	An issue of Condé Nast Traveler	Richard Simmons	Leona Helmsley and Sue Ann Nivens
Audience Demographic	Your dad and the lesbians from next door	male flight attendants and retired stewardesses	middle class housewives who think he's an interior god because he's flamboyant	upper middle class women, gay men and a surprising number of Bears
If you were to hire them, you can expect....	cost overruns. Rarely does Bob come in under budget	charming conversation with lots of trivia. After a few belts of cooking sherry, he'll dish Martha	overuse of a lot of French decorating terms.... and most likely fringe	to be interviewed by one of her people to see if YOU meet her standards
Noted Pluses	nice beard and Sears Craftman spokesman	nice beard and did commercials for Crisco	just a beard	did a guest shot on *Ellen*
Noted Minuses	sued for shoddy workmanship by Conrad Janis, Mindy's Dad on Mork and Mindy	big hair	called Debbie Decorator by his crew and too much chiffon	Kmart

Solution: *Jack first ruled out Christopher Lowell; he really didn't want a princess phone. Bob Vila would be a fine choice, but if the lesbians take care of the construction stuff, Jack can worry about other things. Martha seems like the obvious choice because she does have a large Bear following and is gay friendly. The Kmart tie-in is not a bad thing and really doesn't work against her but she doesn't have a beard....visibly anyway. Burt is the winner. When it gets down to it, Bears are clever enough to furnish their own den without the help of a TV host, however Burt's main topic is a Bear favorite: FOOD. Jack is very happy with his choice.*

CHAPTER FOUR

WHEN A BEAR
NEEDS A BEAR

the social behavior and
sexual habits of the breed
or
"Buy me a shot and I'll hibernate with you"

Six Degrees of Sep-bear-ation

All you need to know is one Bear and you know the whole community

There is an old routine where the gay stand-up comedian says he's from Columbus. Someone says to him, "Oh I know someone gay from Ohio. Maybe you know him." Many straights think that all gays know each other; that there is a network where everyone knows everyone else. This is ludicrous in the gay world as a whole, but in Ursine Society it is not. The community of a minority within a minority is very close-knit and aware of who is doing what to whom and behind whose back. With the advent of the Internet, Bear clubs and frequent flyer miles, Bears know Bears all over the world. Long distance relationships have flourished. New cultures are being learned about. A Bear's libido is helping him make new connections.

The model represented here is but a sample of how Bears know each other.

Frank's Ex is **Ned** *who is married to* **Tom**. **Tom** *and* **Carl** *are both members of Bear Buddies. At the Tool Box,* **Carl** *met* **Peter**, *who knew* **Ned** *from a computer show.* **Ned** *met* **Larry** *through a personal ad in American Bear where* **Larry** *had done a spread. Everyone except his lover,* **Uncle Jack**, *knew* **Larry** *did the spread, including* **Vic**, **Quentin** *and* **Ito**. **Ito** *talks to* **Ed** *on IRC.* **Ed** *has had cyber sex with* **Gary**, *who used to be a third in* **Hank** *and* **Vic**'s *relationship.* **Gary** *has had cyber with* **Steve**. **Steve** *met* **Zeb** *at Gay Mardi Gras.* **Zeb** *serves beers to* **Ollie** *and* **Al**. **Ollie** *and* **Al** *have been together for 5 years.* **Ollie** *has had phone sex with* **Gary** *(basically* **Gary**'s *a whore).* **Al** *was in a Bear contest where he met* **Doug** *backstage.* **Doug** *and* **Ron** *met at* Lazy Bear weekend. **Ron** *and* **Doug** *had a three way with* **Frank** *at a bathhouse, only* **Frank** *never got their names.* **Ron** *still tells* **Gary**, *his sister, how good the sex was with* **Frank**. **Ron** *cruised* **Mike** *in a rest room on 95 while heading north.* **Mike**, *who knows* **Bill** *from all his postings on the BML, is married to* **Carl**. **Bill** *has had a crush on* **Zeb** *since he got a beer from him while on the West Coast for work.* **Bill** *gossips with* **Kevin** *and* **Wally** *via phone but has never met them in person.* **Wally** *has planned a play date with* **Vic**. **Vic** *met* **Jason** *at a Star Trek Convention. Jason has been chatting to* **Quentin** *for years since they were both on CompuServe.* **Jason** *topped* **Peter** *when they met at Folsom St. Fair.* **Jason** *is married to* **Frank**.

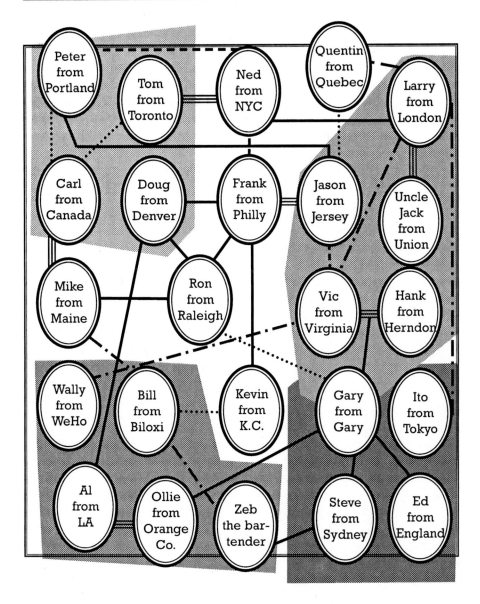

Peter from Portland
Tom from Toronto
Ned from NYC
Quentin from Quebec
Larry from London

Carl from Canada
Doug from Denver
Frank from Philly
Jason from Jersey
Uncle Jack from Union

Mike from Maine
Ron from Raleigh
Vic from Virginia
Hank from Herndon

Wally from WeHo
Bill from Biloxi
Kevin from K.C.
Gary from Gary
Ito from Tokyo

Al from LA
Ollie from Orange Co.
Zeb the bar-tender
Steve from Sydney
Ed from England

Bear slept with Bear
Bear is married to Bear
Bear knows Bear but never met
Bear is an Ex
Bear is sister to Bear

AOL bears4bears room
IRC #bearcave
Bear Bar
Bear Run

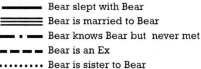

Social Studies

The Social Habits of the Adult Male Bear

A Bear will:

From the beginning man has found it better to be in a pack than alone. This is a means of survival. A social group provides protection, support, fellowship, and at least three other people who share inside jokes. The group or 'sloth' of Bears will consist of a variety of men, each one watching the other one's back— and usually trying to figure out where the knife goes in it. Yes, Bears can often be catty and venomous with wit to their fellow ursine— Bears are, of course, gay men who are notorious for being sharp tongued. However, Bears that often have the nastiest thing to say, say it out of love. A Bear who is willing to jibe his Bear brothers is usually willing to pick him up at the airport or loan him his last few ounces of lube. The dynamic of the Bear group rests on this.

The Bear groups that have formed have mostly formed out of need; a need for companionship, a need for acceptance and mostly a need for touch. Being very tactile, when Bears get together the physical becomes as much a part of the interaction as the verbal. Bears will often rub each other's bellies instead of a handshake. They have no problem giving each other massages at the bar or a hug in the parking lot of the grocery store. They will often stand in a tight circle, arm in arm at gatherings: this is called a Bear scrum, and it occurs with great frequency.

The sense of community within the Bear group is strong. Bears, who have often found themselves to be the outsider most of their lives, yearn to be part of something. They enjoy being part of a team. The whole "gung ho" cheerleader attitude is common among them. Bears send out a strong "comrade" vibe that is easily sensed. That is why a group of Bears is more approachable to a stranger than a clique of twinky club kids. The attitude is just not there, or at least just not visible. The Bears will welcome any new person into the fold. This person is often referred to as Fresh Meat. The Fresh Meat status is kept by the newcomer until he's done most of the local Bears or makes his first joke at another Bear's expense. At this point it is obvious that he has assimilated into the fold of the Bear group.

Shop in pairs

Buy a round of shots

Go out late at night— he is nocturnal

Pick up the check

Have a trickcard ready

Organize a theatre party

Talk to anyone at the bar

Not remember anyone's name

Grope anyone at the bar

Expect to be groped at the bar

Be the first to tell an off color joke

Listen to anyone's troubles

Have the best gossip

Volunteer to drive

Have at least 4 conversations going at once either at a party, in a car or on-line

Work the room

Have slips of papers with phone numbers on them, but he will have no idea to whom the numbers belong

Have a pager, and usually a cell phone

Have a large long distance bill

Date

Mate for life

Mate for life and still date

Often have the nickname "Social Butterfly" or "Julie, your Cruise Director"

The Local Bear Club:
To Join or Not to Join? That is the Question

Joining a formal Bear Club is a personal choice. If you are new to town, freshly out of the closet or haven't been to the bar since the new Bear Club administration had been voted into office, you will be beseeched to join the club. Recruiting new members to the club is intense, and has a somewhat "misery-loves-company" vibe attached to it. But before joining, ask questions and evaluate if the membership dues and hassle are worth the free tee shirt and ten dollars off the local run package.

1 The Founders See if any of these Bears are still around. They most likely have moved on. These are the men that figured if they could have Bear Clubs in Saudi Arabia, we can have one in our town. They started out with fantastic intentions, good connections and worked tirelessly to get the club off the ground. And they did all of that with great devotion. That is until someone didn't agree

with them. Then, like the spoiled child on the playground, they took their marbles and went home. If, however, a founder is still with the club after the second year, he is an old timer. Most do not last that long. When they leave, it will not be a clean break. The original secretary will have conveniently, but accidentally, crashed the mailing list off his hard drive after he's gone.

2 The Current Steering Committee and Administration This is often the group of men who decided they could do it better than the Founders. They wanted to make the club less of a sex thing and more community involved. They worked to get the club non-profit status so they can get a Sam's Club Card.
Be aware: The clubs that really push hard for new members often are doomed by a steering committee that is cliquish. They want members to do the grunt work while they

coast. True, they work for the club, but it is often self serving. The steering committee always has the table by the stage for the Bear contest. One note— if you do join the club, strive to get on to the committee as soon as possible. The position is thankless but powerful: It will be you deciding if it will be chicken or roast beef at the banquet.

3 Dining Out Club If the club has a "Bears Dine Out" group, it is a good test to dine with them to see if you want to join the club. Questions to ask yourself: Is the restaurant they picked one you would have picked or was it Buffet? Did the waitress have noticeable wounds or not speak English? Did the table conversation sparkle with Algonquin Round Table wit or were they re-capping last week's South Park? In the way you answer some of these questions, they may be Bears and you may not.

4 The Club Name and Logo Names that refer to the city without using the city's name are at least somewhat creative. Logos that use clip-art and one of the fonts that came with Office '95 are not. The logo will always be in contention. There are enough graphic designers in the Bear world that each club should have a distinctive and well-designed kick-ass logo. Unfortunately, artists with egos and President's boyfriends who are would-be artists often leave the club with a mark that is uninspired and trite.

5 Unsaid Incest Policy It is never written into the by-laws, but it is a good idea to investigate if the Bears in the club play amongst them-selves. Very often Bears will not play with fellow sisters who are in the club.

6 Club Parties If it's all talk and no action, you may want to just hang around the bar.

7 Use the Internet. Find out what the club's reputation is in other parts of the world. You don't want to be a member of a club that is looked down on. Ask around to see if your hometown club is full of a bunch of the sweetest Bears known to man or if they are viewed as a pack of unfriendly psychos.

8 Joining Procedure Although most clubs have a pay-your-dues-and-show-up-at-the-meetings attitude, there are some clubs that think they are a part of the Greek Fraternal system. New members must be sponsored and go through a pledge process. The rumors of hell week and hazing are mostly exaggerated much to the disappointment of many a pledge.

Either way, you are damned if you join or damned if you don't. Joining can often mean quickly zapping together hors d'oeuvres for a party you were due at 20 minutes ago. Not joining can mean not being invited to the party at all. However maintaining the G.D.I. (God Damn Independent) status does allow you neutrality when the club collapses and a better one is formed.

Bear Clubs

The advantage to having a list of Bear clubs is for personal cultural studies and for hooking up when traveling throughout the United States or abroad. This is the part of the Damron and Spartacus Guide that doesn't exist. If you're looking for a Bear club, they ain't that hard to find.

USA
Alabama
Birmingham
Steel City Centurions
http://members.xoom.com/centurions/

Mobile
Gulf Coast Bears
http://members.aol.com/glfcstbrs/gcb.html

Montgomery
Central Alabama Bears
http://cenalbears.freeservers.com/

Alaska
Anchorage
The Last Frontier Men's Club
http://www.micronet.net/users/~leatherbears/tlfmc.html

Fairbanks
Arctic Bears
http://www.mosquitonet.com/~akbear/arcbears

Arizona
Phoenix
Bears of the Arizona Desert
http://www.bearsazdesert.com

Tucson
Bears of the Old Pueblo
http://www.bear-net.com/bop

Arkansas
Avoca
Ozark Mountain Bears

Rogers
Ozark Mountain Bears

California
Fresno
Golden State Bears
http://home.pacbell.net/
bigbearj/gsb.html

Long Beach
Beach Cities Bears
http://bcb.nikodynamics.com/

Los Angeles
Bears LA
http://www.bearsla.org

Palm Springs
Palm Springs Bears
http://www.palmsprings-
bears.org/
Bears On The Desert

Sacramento
Sacramento Valley Bears
http://www.geocities.com/West
Hollywood/1700

San Diego
Bears San Diego
http://www.bearssd.org

San Francisco
Bears of San Francisco
http://www.bosf.org/

San Jose
South Bay Bears
http://www.southbaybears.org

Santa Rosa
Redwood Empire

Ventura
Bears Ventura
http://www.bearsventura.org

Colorado
Denver
Front Range Bears
http://www.csd.net/~frb

Connecticut
Hartford
Northeast Ursamen, Inc.
http://www.ne-ursamen.org

District of Columbia
**Washington, DC and Balti-
more, MD**
Chesapeake Bay Bears
http://members.aol.com/
ChesBayBrs/

Washington D.C.
The Q Street Bears
http://users.aol.com/qstbears

District of Columbia Bear Club
(DCBC)
http://www.dcbearclub.org/

Florida
Fort Myers
Bears of SouthWest Florida
http://members.aol.com/bears
swf/

Jacksonville
Jacksonville Regional Bear
Association
http://jaxbears.8m.com

Key West
Bone Island Bears
http://www.boneislandbears.
com

Miami
Gen-X Bears South Florida
http://www.genxbears.org/
sflorida

Orlando
The Bears of Central Florida
http://www.bocf.org

Tampa
West Florida Growlers
http://www.westflorida-
growlers.com/

Georgia
Atlanta
Southern Bears
http://www.bearland.com/
southernbears

Hawaii
Honolulu
Hawaii Bear Sanctuary

Aloha Bears
http://welcome.to/alohabears

Idaho
Boise
Bears of Idaho
http://www.idahodesigns.com/
boi/

Illinois
Chicago
Great Lakes Bears-Chicago
http://www.glbears.com

Indiana
Indianapolis
Midwest BearPack
http://members.aol.com/
mwbearpack

Hoosier Bears of Indiana, Inc.
http://www.hoosierbears.org/

Iowa
Iowa City
The Ursine Group (T.U.G)
http://www.iabears.org

Kansas
Topeka
Junction City Teddy Bears
http://members.xoom.com/
grrwoof/default.htm

Wichita
Hirsute Pursuit
http://www.awes.com/hp/

Wichita Bears
http://www.bear.net/clubs/
wichita.bears/

Kentucky
Lexington
Moonshine Bears of Kentucky
http://members.aol.com/
dreamrbear/mnshine.htm

Louisiana
New Orleans
New Orleans Bear & Bear Trapper Social Club http://mem-
bers.aol.com/
nobbtsc

Maine
Bangor
Mainely Bears

Portland
Bare Bears of Maine
http://www.barebears.com/

Massachusetts
Boston
New England Bears
http://www.nebears.org

Gen-X Bears Boston
http://www.genxbears.org/
boston

Fitchburg
Monty Bears

New Bedford
Bay State Bears
community.webtv.net/ameri-
canearcub/welcometo

Michigan
Detroit
Motor City Bears
http://www.motorcitybears.com

Grand Rapids
Lake Michigan Bears
http://www.geocities.com/West
Hollywood/Park/3769/

Traverse City
North West Michigan

Minnesota
Twin Cities
North Country Bears
http://www.ncbears.com/

Mississippi
Jackson
Cotton Pickin' Bears of Mississippi
http://www.intop.net/~cpbears

Missouri
Kansas City
The Kansas City Cave Bears
http://www.geocities.com/West
Hollywood/Village/6630/index.
htm

St. Louis
Show Me Bears
http://gaystl.com/smb

Nebraska
Omaha
Flat Water Bears
http://www.geocities.com/
flatwaterbears

Nevada
Las Vegas
BlackJack Bears of Las Vegas
http://www.blackjackbears.org

Reno
Comstock Grizzlies
http://comstockgrizzlies.gay.
web1000.com/

New Mexico
Albuquerque
Bears of Mañana
http://www.thuntek.net/~kbear
/bom/bom.htm

New York
Albany
STARS M.C. http://www.wiz-
vax.net/starsmc/

Buffalo
Buffalo Bears http://
buffalobears.buffnet.net/

New York City
MetroBears New York
http://www.metrobears.org/

Long Island Bears
http://home.earthlink.net/
~davidjb7

North Carolina
Asheville
Blue Ridge Bears
http://www.blueridgebears.org

Raleigh
Carolina Bear Lodge
http://www.carolinabears.com/

Ohio
Cincinnati
River Bears, Cincinnati
http://homepages.gayweb.com
/riverbears/

Cleveland
ARKTOS
http://home.neo.rr.com/arktos/

Cleveland Bears
http://members.aol.com/
clevebears/bearclub.html

Columbus
Columbus Ursine Brotherhood
(CUB)
http://www.infinet.com/~cub

Dayton
Brotherhood Of Bears, Dayton,
OH, Inc.
http://www.geocities.com/west
hollywood/stonewall/8249

Oklahoma
Oklahoma City
Red Earth Bears
http://www.redearthbears.org/

Oregon
Portland
Oregon Bears
http://www.oregonbears.org/

Gen-X Bears Oregon Chapter

http://www.geocities.com/West
Hollywood/Village/3714/
genxor.html

Pennsylvania
Harrisburg
Susquehanna Valley Bears
http://www.geocities.com/west
hollywood/stonewall/3514

Pittsburgh
Burgh Bears
http://www.spdcc.com/home/
burghbears

Tennessee
Chattanooga
Lookout Bears
http://members.xoom.com/
LookoutBears/

Johnson City
Tri Cities Bears
http://www.homestead.com/
etbearclub/TCBhome.html

Knoxville
Appalachian Bear Club
http://www.geocities.com/West
Hollywood/8497

Memphis
Memphis Bears
http://bigfoot.com/
~memphisbears

Nashville
Music City Bears
http://www.musiccitybears.com

Texas
Austin
Heart of Texas Bears (HOT
Bears)
http://www.heartoftexasbears.
org/

Dallas
Dallas Bears
http://www.dallasbears.org/

Houston
Houston Area Bears
http://www.houstonareabears.
com/

Utah
Salt Lake City
Wasatch Mountain Bears
http://www.geocities.com/
~wmbears/

Washington
Seattle
Renegade Bears
http://www.renegadebears.org

Gen-X Bears: Western Washington
http://clubs.yahoo.com/clubs/
genxbearswesternwashington

Northwest Bears
http://www.nwbears.org/

Movie Bear Cinema
http://www.websitesnw.com/
cinema/index.html

Tacoma
Evergreen State

West Virginia
Charleston
Mountain State Bears

Wisconsin
Eau Claire
Chippewa Valley Bears
http://cvbears.bearden.net/

Brew City Bears
http://www.brewcitybears.org

Superior (also Duluth MN)
BackWoods Bears
http://www.win.bright.net/
~docmac/bwb.html

CANADA
Alberta
Calgary
Bearback Calgary
http://www.bearbackcalgary.
com/

Edmonton
Alternative Bears of Edmonton
http://plaza.powersurfr.com/
OUTlines/altbears

B.E.A.R.S. of Edmonton and
Area Recreational Society
http://www.freenet.edmonton.
ab.ca/~bears

British Columbia
Kelowna
Okanagan Bears (OK Bears)
http://www.okbears.com/http:/
/www.okbears.com

Vancouver
BC Bears Society
http://www.bcbears.com/

Manitoba
Winnipeg
Manitoba Bears
http://www.escape.ca/~akoc/
bears2.html

New Brunswick
Fredericton
East Coast Bears
http://personal.nbnet.nb.ca/
lairbear/

Ontario
London
Forest City Bears
http://www.gaycanada.com/
fcbears/

North Bay
Northern Ontario Bears
http://www.geocities.com/West
Hollywood/Village/1835

Ottawa
Ottawa Bears / Ours Ottawa
http://www.gayottawa.com/
bears

Toronto
Bear Buddies Toronto
http://www.torque.net/~bbt

Québec
Montréal
Ours Montréal / Montreal Bears
http://www.mtl-ours-bears.qc.ca/

EUROPE
AUSTRIA:
Vienna
Wiener Runde
http://www.austrianbears.gay.at/

BELGIUM:
Brussels
G&M Belgium
http://www.biggerworld.com/

FINLAND:
Helsinki
Fin-Bears
http://www.saunalahti.fi/~mscfin/bear/fbsite.html

GERMANY:
Cologne
BEARS COLOGNE
http://www.bearscologne.de/

BERGBÄREN
http://www.bergbaeren.de/

Mannheim
Mannheim Bären Treff
(Mannheim Bears)
http://www.geocities.com/westhollywood/heights/2125/mannbear.html

Pfundskerle Girth & Mirth Südwest
http://www.pfundskerle.de/

Munich
Munich Bears
http://www.munich-bears.de

Isar Bears
http://www.isarbears.de/

IRELAND:
Dublin

LUBE - Leather Uniform Bear Encounter Group - Ireland
http://gofree.indigo.ie/~lube

ITALY:
Milano
Magnum Club Italia
http://magnumclub.freeservers.com/

SWEDEN:
Stockholm
Viking Bears
http://www.geocities.com/westhollywood/9688

SWITZERLAND:
Zürich
XLarge
http://www.xlarge.ch/

Swiss Bears
http://members.xoom.com/swissbears

TURKEY:
Ankara
Bears of Turkey
http://www.geocities.com/WestHollywood/Stonewall/7788

UNITED KINGDOM:
London
BearHug
http://www.bearhug.net/

Lines & Bears
http://members.aol.com/linesbears/

Bears 2000
http://www.bears2000.org.uk/

Manchester
PAWS Bear Club
http://www.bigfoot.com/~pawsbearclub

Newcastle upon Tyne
BONE (Bears of the North East)
www.florentine.demon.co.uk/bone

Sheffield
teds chubs & chasers

AUSTRALIA
Brisbane
Sunbears - BrisBears on the Sunshine Coast
http://www.geocities.com/WestHollywood/4840/

Canberra
BearsCanberra
http://www.webone.com.au/~bearscan

Melbourne
VicBears Inc.
http://www.geocities.com/vicbears

Sydney
Harbour City Bears
http://www.hcbears.com/

Sydney Bears
http://www.ozemail.com.au/~colwellr/sydneybears/

EXOTIC OTHERS
SOUTH AFRICA:
Port Elizabeth
Ibhayi Bears
http://www.bigfoot.com/~ibhayibears

JAPAN:
Tokyo
Bear Club Japan
http://www.st.rim.or.jp/~lonestar/bcj/

ARGENTINA:
Buenos Aires
Osos de Buenos Aires
http://www.mundogay.com/ososmain.htm

CHILE:
Santiago
Club de Osos Chilenos
http://www.geocities.com/ososchilenos

MEXICO:
Ciudad de Mexico
Osos Mexicanos
http://www.ososmexicanos.com.mx/

Bear clubs have sprouted up in all corners of the globe, however sometimes as soon as they sprout they wither and die. Therefore, this list has the potential to be outdated between the time you buy the book and the time you get home to read it. The most up-to-date list of Bear clubs can be found in one of two places: the Internet at www.resourcesforbears.com (although remember the website message mentioned on page 66) or in a bi-monthly periodical geared specifically for Bear men, such as <u>Bear</u> or <u>American Bear</u>.

Who's Who in the Bear Club

1 The Treasurer- He's held the position for years and is the only one in the club with a decent credit rating. His other half is an active club member and his flatbed was used for the float in the last Pride Parade.

2 The Secretary- He has a laptop and full computer system at home, making him not only the secretary, but also the club's web-master. Those in the club who don't really like him become his best friend as soon as their hard drive crashes.

3 The Social Director- A recent reject from Betty Ford, he has connections at the beer distributor and works in the food service industry.

4 The Trophy- He's been to several Bear Events and has brought home the sashes. He is who everyone points to as the epito-me of a Bear. He'll have a full Beard, full belly, be butch, and be a bottom.

5 The President- Got his position by sleep-ing with everyone in the club and came up with one idea that sounded good on paper. He won't do a whole lot the rest of his term except dress as Santa for the Christmas Party.

6 The Ex-Club Member- After 3 years of putting up with all the politics and holding at least two elected offices, he quit. He still, however, stays in contact with the members and crashes parties. He does make a killer pasta salad, so his attendance is over-looked at the pool party.

7 The Local Lesbian- She really can't stand the local dyke bar and has found a home at the local Bear bar. She is on the Bears softball team and fields better than 4 of the guys. She is into leather and watch-ing two guys together because "guys know how to have sex."

8 The Ghost- Everyone knows his face and has talked about him. He never was a mem-ber and comes to the bar infrequently. When he does come, he sits alone and waits to be approached. He's either shy or aloof, but rarely goes home alone. Anyone who has been with him, speaks highly of him, but aren't sure of his name.

9 The Community Liaison- Not an elected post, but an important one. He talks fre-quently in Bear chat rooms and knows Bears in other parts of the world. He is a health care worker and is responsible for making the big checks at Kinko's for chari-ty events.

10 The Dancer- His time at the bar or any club party is spent on the dance floor. His personality exists only there, however he does have a good butt.

11 The Vice President- He does all the work and knows all the names and num-bers of all the club members and even the Bears at the local bar who aren't members. Got the position because he has a hot tub.

The Bear Bar
A place to call home

The local watering hole for the Bear is welcoming, accepting and usually doesn't have much lighting. Unlike the typical gay bar, Bear bars have little need for pastels and ferns, but instead rely on the local Army Navy store for their interior decorating. Theming is clutch in the Bear bar. Country and Western, Garage or an All Black Industrial motif are most apropos. Wicker is seldom used. If you are exploring a new city, this list of criteria of that which creates the proper Bear bar atmosphere, will help in finding the correct drinking establishment. And if all else fails, try the Eagle: there's one in almost every city.

Have	Have Not
A double entendre name: The ToolBox, The Chute, and The ManHole	A tropical name like Key West, The Copa or anything that is remotely French sounding
Walls covered with black and white posters of other Bear bars	Walls covered with Nagel Prints
Wood and metal	Black lacquer and chrome
A George Strait Neon Beer sign	Neon palm tree and flamingo
A small shop that sells poppers and cockrings (although in Texas, cockrings will be sold as napkin rings)	A bathroom attendant with a variety of cologne samples (although in South Beach the cologne will be on tap)
A bartender that has tight jeans, a moustache and an off color joke	A bartender that has a tank top, shaved armpits and attitude
A trophy case with various civic awards and club memorabilia	A wall of mirrors

The Lone Star Saloon

Boasting an almost mythical status is the Lone Star Saloon. It is the Mecca to which Bears make their pilgrimage. Being in the center of the Gay universe, otherwise known as San Francisco, this rather small tavern has garnered a reputation for Bears, Bikers and Mayhem, even though that reputation may be self imposed and on their matchbooks. Be aware that there is a line to get in during IBR and plan to be intimate once inside. Not that this will be a romance but because the crowd inside is packed so tight you could be getting groped but not know by whom. Due to California's no smoking policy, the back courtyard is where you should be careful not to forget your asthma inhaler.

The Bear Bar Checklist

Below are listed some Bear Bars around the world. This handy list is for you to keep track of the number of bars you've traveled to and most likely stumbled out of. They are in order of their airport codes because you will have to fly to most of them. Get your flight attendant friend to help translate if need be.

There is also a space for you to fill in comments about the bar, e.g., the bar stools are too small, the bartender is cute or the name and number of the trick you went home with.

City	Bear Bar	Runners Up	Comments
ABQ	◇The Ranch		
AMS	◇Argos	◇Cuckoos Nest	
ATL	◇The Eagle	◇Hoedown's	
AUS	◇Chain Drive		
BWI	◇The Eagle		
BCN	◇The Eagle	◇El Horno	
BTR	◇George's Place		
TXL	◇Connection	◇Knast	
BOS	◇119 Merrimac	◇Boston Ramrod	
BUF	◇Buddies		
BHM	◇The Tool Box		
BNE	◇Sportsman Hotel		
CLT	◇The Brass Rail		
CRW	◇The Tap Room		
ORD	◇Cell Block	◇Touche	
CVG	◇Shooters	◇Spurs	
CLE	◇The Leather Stallion	◇The Eagle	
CMH	◇Trade Winds II	◇The Eagle in Exile	
CPH	◇The Men's Bar		
DFW	◇The Eagle	◇The Hidden Door	
DEN	◇Wrangler		
EAU	◇The Wolfe's Den		
EDI	◇Central Bar	◇The New Town	
FLL	◇Chaps	◇The Ramrod	
BDL	◇Nick's Café		
HEL	◇Cafe Bar Escale		
HOU	◇Nighthawks		
MCI	◇The Dixie Belle	◇Side Kicks	
CGN	◇Zipp's		
LPA	◇Bärenhöhle		
LAS	◇The Buffalo	◇The Eagle	
LEX	◇Crossings		

LHR	◇The Kings Arms	◇Duke's
LAX	◇Pistons	◇The Faultline
MAN	◇The Rembrant	◇Chains
MEL	◇The Laird	◇The Star
MEM	◇The Pipeline	
MIA	there are no real Bear Bars in Miami, only bars where disco bunnies let their chest hair grow in for a week	
MKE	◇The Boot Camp	
MSP	◇The Eagle	
YUL	◇LeStud	
BNA	◇The Chute	
MSY	◇Rawhide 2010	◇The Phoenix
LGA	◇Ty's	◇The Dugout
MCO	◇The Full Moon	◇Hank's
CDG	◇The One Way	◇The Bear's Den
PHX	◇NuTowne	◇Boot Camp
PHL	◇The Bike Stop	
PDX	◇The Dirty Duck	
PVD	◇Yukon Trading Co	◇The Eagle
RDU	◇FLEX	
SMF	◇FLEX	
STL	◇The Bolt	
SAN	◇Zone	◇Wolfs
SFO	◇The Lone Star	◇Daddy's
SEA	◇Cuffs	
SYD	◇The Beresford Hotel	
NRT	◇Kuma no ashiato	
YYZ	◇The Toolbox	◇Black Eagle
TUS	◇The Venture-N	
YVR	◇The Royal Pub	◇Chuck's Pub
IAD	◇The Eagle	

When Good Bars Go Bad

Bars are transitory. Rarely does one have an existence longer than the trend on which it was opened. Usually it's because the owners change, but sometimes it's because management wants to go after a new crowd. Bear bars, as a rule, do have a longer life than most twink bars. Having a clientele that is obviously not the most fashion conscious means that Bears will tend to be less fickle and thus stay with their home bar. This does not mean that Bear bars are not at risk. The worst case scenario for change is when the Bear bar wants to attract a younger, hipper, more club kid crowd. Any good conversation the bar had will go out the window and a pungent aroma of CKOne will penetrate the air.

The Bear Run Weekend

The Bear Run Weekend is oddly named because no one really runs at these events. Bears as a rule are not known for their speed. They swagger, sashay, strut and cruise, but they do not run. That is unless it is away from the freaky guy who has a thing for pantyhose and Celine Dion. And it is also not just a weekend. Because Bears will travel a great distance to these events, a large number of them arrive early. The weekend prior to the official run weekend is when the foreigners arrive. You can always count on the Australians and the Japanese being in the host city a week early and traveling the U.S. after the event. It is not uncommon for them and the Europeans, that show up at least the Monday before the run, not to have specific plans post-run in hopes of catching themselves a Bear in the States for a few days. On Wednesday, the Bears that live farther than 500 miles from the host city, will appear late in the night but early enough to make last call at the bar. Thursday is really the kick off for most Bear events although registration most likely won't occur till Friday. Thursday is the day out-of-town Bears get to know the city. The local Bear club will plan a non-run-package trip to a local attraction. The attraction will involve food in some way. That night the local bar will have a special party for early Bears and it is notoriously the best night of the run. Everyone is getting to know one another, previous run participants are catching up with friends they haven't seen since last year, and everyone is sizing each other up and figuring out how they are going to fit all these men into their schedule over the next 72 hours.

Festivals Throughout the Year

Get out that daytimer and book rooms weeks, if not months in advance for these events. The following runs have proven to be popular and have sustained longer than their inaugural run. The beauty of these events is that, due to their intimacy, they lend themselves to a more bonding experience and bondaging experience if that's what you're into. (There are Bears known to travel with portable sling apparati or barber chairs.)

Bears Going Down

When looking for a room, try to get a low floor in the host hotel. Elevators move slowly, and although the thought of being pressed like a sardine into one with big hairy men is enticing, the novelty wears off quickly. And remember, there is a weight limit on those things.

What's the clever name?	When does it happen?	Where am I flying to?	Who's putting it on?	Why should I go?
Fiesta de los Osos	January	Tuscon	Bears of the Old Pueblo	Whacking the Piñata takes on a whole new meaning.
Texas Bear Round-Up	late March or early April	Dallas	Dallas Bears	To see if the statement about all things being big in Texas is true.
Spring Thaw	April	Seattle	Cascade Bears	The Gaslight Inn alone is worth the trip.
Bear All	Early July	Atlanta	Southern Bears	Atlanta + July = Naked
Bear Camp	Early July	near Hinkley, Minnesota	North Country Bears	Hairy men camping in the woods has porn story written all over it.
Lazy Bear Weekend	Mid July	Guerneville, California	Sacramento Valley Bears	Wallowing in the Russian River
The Great Canadian Bear Hunt	Late July	Toronto	Bear Buddies Toronto	Playing with foreign Bears from a distant mystical country called Canada
Bear & Southern Decadence	Around Labor Day Weekend	New Orleans	New Orleans Bears & Bear Trapper Social Club	"Show us your tits" becomes "Show us your hairy tits"
LeBear Day Weekend	Labor Day Weekend	Milwaukee	Brew City Bears	Bear and beer— 'nuff said
Octobearfest	Early October	Denver	Front Range Bears	You can also pay homage to Alexis Morel Carrington Colby Dexter while you're there.
Hibearnation	November	St. Louis	Show Me Bears	Because Judy Garland immortalized that town. Meet her there, dammit!
Bear Invasion	November	Washington D.C.	D.C. Bear Club	You could be mentioned in the next Starr Report

The Triple Crown

Attending just one of these three events in any given year could damage (or enhance) your reputation. Attend two of the three, and people will definitely be talking. Three for three— slut! Yet each of these fine events offers a unique aspect of the Bear experience:

International Bear Rendezvous
San Francisco,
Presidents' Day Weekend

This event has ties to all aspects of the gay community. It is not uncommon for drag queens to come to the Lone Star during IBR, however it is doubtful that her fake boobs will fit in the cramped bar, let alone her big hair. The Bears of San Francisco bring in comedians, impersonators, d.j.'s, and singing groups but the big event is the big pageant. The International Mr. Bear contest is taken very seriously here. Sash queen wannabes: brush up on your "how I can make the world a better place" speech; audience, be prepared for a long show!

Bear Pride Chicago
Memorial Day

Starting out as Big & Bear Weekend, sponsored by Girth & Mirth Chicago and Great Lakes Bears, and coinciding with International Mr. Leather weekend, Bear Pride eventually evolved into the most urban of the Bear events and the highest attended. Chicago, home to corn-fed husky boys, hosts the official summer kick-off party, and nothing says summer fun like flannel shirts, chaps and the inner city. Notorious for always needing a new host hotel

each year, the lobby and halls fill with hairy horny men, some of them in little more than boxers and a leather vest.

Bear Bust Orlando
Sometime in October

Bears of Central Florida hosts the most rural of these Bear events, although it's really quite suburban. Held in an atmosphere that is part backwoods swamp and part 50's motel, and at a time of year when the rest of the nation is getting ready for hibernation, Bear Bust obviously pulls the men to Orlando. Let's not forget that Otown is also the home to a plethora of amusement parks, and with many a Bear also involved in ACE (American Coaster Enthusiasts), the draw to the Bust is irresistible. The Disney influence is obvious, as the event will have a theme.

Miss UrsaKitt says:

"Never wear the tee shirt you get at the run until you get back home. Otherwise you may be wearing the same shirt as someone else at the run. And when two bitches wear the same outfit at the party, someone could get bruised."

The Bear Weekend Time Clock

A look at what you'll typically be doing and when

Friday

2:30 Cut out of work early after getting in late. You were out until 2am on Thursday night at the local Bear bar for a Bon Voyage Party.

3:30 Quickly pack because you waited 'til the last minute. Rummage in closet for the Spike tee shirt that has the nipple areas cut out and pray it still fits.

4:46 Arrive at airport for 4:50 flight. At gate you learn of a delay and head to the bar.

5:57 Meet other Bears, David from San Francisco and David from LA, connecting in your city on the way to the event. You consider a quick three-way in the showers at the Admiral's Club.

5:08 Order 4th Fuzzy Navel and buy a shot for your new friends.

5:30 Boarding announcement is made— you and your new friends size up the flight crew. You decide to give flight attendant Nancy grief. The armrests grab your ass— after this weekend, you will diet— you swear.

8:27 Two beers and a screwdriver later, you land.

You and the other bears have wrecked Nancy. You only had carry-on but you go to baggage claim to cruise— plenty of Bears are showing up in the airport.

9:13 Taxi to the host hotel.

9:40 Bags are tossed into room and you're off to registration where you get your run package and the phone number of the check-in guy, also named David.

10:50 Run into the guy you lusted after at the last Bear run, a couple who wants you for a three-way and get an invite to an after-hours party hosted by the local leather club.

12:06 Beer has become the drink of choice and you realize you skipped lunch and dinner.

12:58 A local Bear and his friend invite you to an all night diner. The chili cheese fries are the last ones you will eat because you are going on that diet after this weekend. You need to stop at an ATM.

1:22 You spend the night with the local Bear's friend because he had a tight butt and good forearms, but he had been with the local Bear earlier and couldn't complete the job. You both fall asleep in your room at **3:15** to the glow of Comedy Central on cable.

Saturday

9:30 Eye-opener cocktail party sponsored by the local Bear club— they serve Bloody Marys but you sleep through it.

10:50 You decide to get up as your trick is getting

What you shouldn't forget to pack...

Condoms and Lube
(although both will most likely be included in the run pack)

Altoids
(good for breath and for blow jobs)

T-Shirt from the last Bear run you attended
(to be worn to the Thursday night party so that other Bears can know where they've seen you before)

New Trick Cards
(the old ones have your old e-mail address or your ex-lover's name)

Laptop
(because you need to keep abreast of the BML and e-mail)

Portable Blender
(the room with a blender is the room where the party is)

Baseball Cap
(the one with your AOL handle stitched onto the front. To be worn at the on-line party.)

dressed. That's when you decide to ask his name. It's David.

11:30 Lobby of the hotel— you try to find someone to go to brunch with. So is everyone else. The local Bear you ate with last night is organizing a caravan to a great Chinese joint just outside of town. You decline and instead head to the bar that's hosting a Saturday T dance

12:00 Side trip to the local convenience store to load up on room supplies— Diet Coke and Barbecue Pringles.

12:47 You've met most of these Bears before and have had sex with a lot of them. Your bar banter is mostly catching up on who is with whom this weekend. Jack Daniel's shots are done frequently.

1:14 After being groped on the way to the bathroom, you make a dinner date with a guy who knows a great little all-you-can-eat BBQ place. Word spreads and soon 17 guys decide to go too.

2:26 YMCA comes over the speakers, your shirt comes off and your hands wave over your head. You take to the dance floor to dance with a cub you've been eyeing all day.

5:39 AOL party in the Hawaiian Room at the host hotel. No one looks like their GIF and their voices are a higher pitch than you expected.

7:00 The number of dining companions has risen to 22 and they're all waiting in the lobby for you. You were at the ATM again.

7:37 The little BBQ place closes after running out of ribs and pulled pork.

9:00 Bear Contest at the Eagle. You have slept with at least 2 contestants in each category. Kamikazes are on special.

10:40 The contest is running too long, the MC is drunk but entertaining and you flirt with one guy who has on only a jock strap and another guy who looks like your high school civics teacher.

11:05 All three of you end up in the hot tub at the hotel.

11:08 All bathing suits are off.

11:10 You all head to one of their rooms.

12:20 You wash up and leave them together— they are both named David, oddly enough.

12:46 You cruise past the other Bears' rooms— many of them decorated with lights, flags, stuffed teddy bears and dildos.

1:39 You stumble into at least three of those rooms.

2:12 You meet up with the David from check-in and both of you head to the private leather party.

2:22 Too much attitude for you but David decides to stay. You get to your room alone. You order a pizza from the 24 hour joint listed in your run package.

3:30ish In a stupor, you answer the knock at your door. It's the cub you were eyeing. He's lost, shirtless and apologetic.

Sunday

10:00 You're the first at the eye-opener cocktail party. President of the local Bear club comments on your haircut. He has a barber fetish.

12:21 Club and Vendor Fair is already busy. You purchase the new Bear sex video, three tee shirts and a pair of shorts. The hairy guy selling raffle tickets talks you into buying two floor-to-crotch strips. He does feels your cock. You need to hit an ATM again.

2:55 Happy Hour For Bears cocktail party, sponsored by the local AIDS organization. The ribbon is pinned to you by a guy who grabs you and rubs your chest. He offers to buy you a shot of Goldschlager.

3:15 Back in your room you two cuddle and kiss the afternoon away while watching "Murder on the Orient Express" on AMC.

5:45 He announces his lover is expecting him for dinner.

7:00 Bon Voyage Banquet and you choose the chicken. You see the guys who won the titles at the contest and finally catch up with David from San Francisco and David from LA (the two guys you met on the plane). They met a guy and spent the whole weekend in bed.

11:15 Closing party at the bar. You realize you have not taken one picture nor traded a trick card with anyone.

Sash Queens
The Mr. Bear Competitions

One of the expected highlights of the Bear Weekend is the Bear Beauty Pageant. Like the Miss USA, it has a swimsuit competition. Like Miss America, it has an eveningwear competition. And like the Oscars, it goes on too long!

Being crowned Mr. Bear Something or Other is the dream in every queer little cub's heart. Competition is fierce. The number of contestants vying for the coveted title can be upwards of twenty-five. Each and every one of them hopes to wear the tiara. But as stiff as the competition is, brotherhood reigns supreme backstage where each Bear is said to help his fellow Bear fluff up for their moment in the spotlight. As it has been said, "It's not who wins, but the friendships that are made." The categories for which the men are fighting:

Mr. Grizzly - The Bear most likely to win everyone's hearts. He will be fit, but big. Beard- thick and auburn. Eveningwear- leather jock strap, black boots and leather vest. Swimwear- he loses the vest and boots. Talent- he'll tilt his head back and dart his tongue into the air. Interview Answer- "I'm just looking for Mr. Right, and that's my husband in the audience."

Daddy Bear or Mr. Polar Bear - This is for the Bear man who is past his prime but still looks good. Will have a round, prominent belly. Most likely to be a late bloomer into the gay world or ex clergy. Eveningwear- anything goes: his costume will be outrageous and may have moving parts. Swimwear- he will have no shame and wear a novelty jockstrap with a blinking light. Interview Answer- "I never met a cub I haven't bought dinner for."

Mr. Cub - he will be hairless and barely have a goatee. Eveningwear- jeans and a tee shirt- he has very little imagination. Swimwear- a Speedo and it will be well packed. Talent- a Speedo and it will be well packed. Interview Answer- "My fantasy is to be stuck in a log cabin with a Bear and snuggle all night in front of the fireplace." To which the crowd will ooh and aah.

Mr. International Bear- This winner comes from San Francisco's IBR. He will be the most devoted of winners and take his title very seriously. He will also be the source of controversy as although he will be *Mr. International Bear*, it is rare that he will be from outside of the U.S.

Other Noteworthy Events

Mac World

Held sometime in early August. Show a Bear technology and a Bear will be happy. Put him in a convention center full of technology and he will shit himself. Mac Computers have long been the preferred brand of Bears (and Drew Carey for that matter), so when Steve Jobs, the head of Apple, shows off his new stuff, expect there to be Bears on hand. It should be noted that the technology is taking precedence here and not the libido. If a big hairy man asks how big your hard drive is, he's looking for an answer in megs not inches.

Ethnic Festivals

It could be a Festival Italiano, Highland Days at the Park, Octoberfest or even a picnic at the Russian Orthdox Church. Two things will be there: Food and Bears. And those two things go so well together. Scottish festivals are good for looking up kilts, and the Germans will have good (and a lot of) beer, but the food at these events is why Bears go. Usually made by old women who still speak their native tongue even though they've been in the U.S. for decades, it's made fresh and served cheap. Cruising factor is low, although the old women's husbands are usually Bears and she's been too busy in the kitchen.

Gay Day at Disney

Not a Bear event, but a shindig that should not be missed. Given that most Bears have a keen awareness of their inner child, they realize that he must be treated to the biggest playground of them all. Held in June during Gay Pride Month, the Magic Kingdom is overrun with twinks, dykes, trolls, queens and fairies: and we ain't talking Tinkerbell here. To turn this into a Bear event, be sure to get Baloo's autograph in Adventureland, Woof at some of the Pirates in the Caribbean, and gather with fellow Bears at the Country Bear Jamboree at 1:00 pm. Try to figure out who most looks like Big Al.

Winnie the Pooh Part 3 Disney Version

Disney took the cute little story of the Bear with Very Little Brain and made him lucrative. Little did Walt realize that Winnie the Pooh would be 2nd only to Mickey in the merchandising cast...and we know who's buying it all! Gay Bears have looked to Pooh as an icon of the idealized existence— to be housed in the 100 acre wood, feast on honey and have true friends that will pull you out of a hole when needed. Also, Pooh wears a red shirt: the symbol of unity worn among homosexuals on Gay Day at the Magic Kingdom.

Fantasy Life
SciFi vs. Ren

In high school, it may be called the D&D Club, Parallox or The Organians, but they are still the Nerd and Geek Society. And you will find a cub or two in there. Post-graduation, there are Bears still belonging to such organizations, only they meet in comic book stores and not that "certain" English teacher's classroom.

Being that a rich imagination is a hallmark of any gay man, a fantasy life that is not filled with go-go boys, but warlocks, wizards and phasers is common among Bears. Divided into two camps, there are Ren Bears who attend Renaissance Festivals and SciFi Bears who frequent Star Trek Conventions.

The Ren Bear often has straggly hair and beard, a tattoo that looks like something off a Led Zeppelin album cover and at least one piece of jewelry that is a dragon. He has outgrown his Frodo Lives tee shirt, but that doesn't prevent him from wearing it. His leather mug rarely has beer, but natural sarsaparilla or some other "potion." He goes by the nickname Ogre and speaks in rhyme and incantations.

The Renaissance Festival
Most times hosted by the Society for Creative Anachronism, The Ren Faire Circuit has almost as heavy a calendar as Bear runs. These trips back to medieval life are held at vineyards or cow pastures and it will rain, so the ground will be muddy. They are rife with Bears and the stench of smoking meats. Beards are a must and Bears pop up throughout the Faire as the King, the Blacksmithe, or the Muckraker. Only the fittest bears will be in the Joust and the biggest queen will be the Court Jester.

The SciFi Bear typically has a conservative, yet out-of-date wardrobe and a satellite dish because his cable company doesn't carry the SciFi Channel. He camped out in line all week for the premier of Episode One and brought his programming/tech support job with him via cell phone and laptop. He has a website dedicated to Commander Riker and links to Trekkers all over the world. He thought the infamous "Star Trek Convention" skit on Saturday Night Live was funny but didn't really see the irony in it.

The Star Trek Conventions
In any city at any time of the year there could be a Trekker convention. Held at a local Sheraton, Bears get all dolled up as Klingons and parade around the lobby holding battle rallies. Cruising does not occur during the rally, but it does in the vendor fair. *"If you wanna try on that Borg costume, you'll have to come up to my room where I have one in your size" (wink wink)*. Still, Bears are not usually there to get laid— they're there to discuss and debate the future of the Starfleet Academy and the Federation. Live Long and Prosbear.

Fantasy Bears*

Scotty *Star Trek*
Commander Riker *STNG*
Worf *STNG*
Arthur *Excalibur*
Llug *Willow*
Captain Jack *Babylon 5*
Zzeben *Conan*

*not in the bedroom

Don We Now Our *Gay* Apparel

Christmas Time for Bears

That special time of year when everybody becomes a kid again doesn't exclude Bear men. In fact it almost seems like a custom made holiday for Bears. First off, it's cold in most places, so cuddling by the fire in warm flannel shirts is appropriate. Second, there's the food: Christmas cakes, cookies and of course, eggnog. Third - Decorating! What Bear man hasn't had that elusive dream of turning his front yard into a winter wonderland complete with a glowing baby Jesus. That is until his other half insists on a Victorian theme for the tree. And finally, there's the visit from Santa Claus to stuff your stocking.

SANTAS 'ROUND THE WORLD

Bringing joy to little children and big men from Amsterdam to Zanzibar. This right jolly old elf is the perfect example of the Polar Bear type of man. He is a prototype of the Bear: good hearted, a bit hefty and a full beard. No Christmas party is complete without him and whoever gets to play him gets all those hot bodies in their lap! Bear men often earn extra cash around the holidays playing Santa, however the thought of snotty nosed rug rats ruining the red velvet pants is repulsive.

Australia	Saint Nick
Switzerland	Samichlaus
Sweden	Jultomten
Finland	Joulipukki
Spain	The Three Magi
Canada	Belsnickle
Netherlands	Sinter Klaas
France	Pere Noel
England	Father Christmas
Denmark	Kris Kringle
Czech Republic	Saint Nicholas
Germany	Weinachtsmann

Watching in a Winter Wonderland

Rankin and Bass, the wizards of puppet animation holiday specials, gave us a wonderful image of the King Bear every year. *Santa Claus is Coming to Town* explains the history of Santa and starts him as a young buck being raised by little bearded men in the woods. He grows a red beard that turns white with time and he goes on to become a legend. *The Year Without a Santa Claus* gave us the unforgettable Heat and Snow Miser songs and Santa makes a bedridden appearance because he's sick. This is the weakest Santa, but he's still a Bear. Mrs. Claus dresses up as Santa, so she's a Bear and the Heat Miser has Bear qualities too. *Rudolph the Red-Nosed Reindeer* has a thin Santa that Mama Claus is trying to fatten up, but the real stars are Burl Ives as the narrating snowman and Yukon Cornelius, a woodsman/trapper. Yukon saves Rudolph from a big hairy beast called a Bumble (they bounce, you know). And because Herbie the elf, who wants to be a dentist, removes all of Bumble's teeth, Yukon and Bumble live together happily ever after. Burl Ives is the perfect Snow Bear with a white Balboa and squinty eyes. He also scores big points because he was the inspiration for Al's Snowman character in the *Home Improvement* clay animation Christmas special (and anything that has to do with Al Borland has to be good).

Deck the Halls with Chains and Handcuffs
fa la la la la la la la la

In an effort to make it on both Santa's Naughty and Nice lists, a bunch of butch little elves festooned in black leather kick off the holiday season. **Santa Saturday** is the annual after-Thanksgiving escape, just when you're getting sick of leftover turkey and the family you're visiting. This festive afternoon is a crossover event that is heavily attended by Bears even though The Bucks Motorcycle Club sponsors it. Held in New Hope, Pennsylvania, this charity event is like a mini Bear run, complete with a show, beer, food, and as a bonus, a photo session with an S&M Santa. The popular pose is not sitting on his lap but being spanked over it. The crowd is mostly the leather community, so expect to see wreaths hanging from nipple rings and VW Bugs in the parking lot. Arrive early because attendance is high even though the event is not overly publicized.

Games Bears Play
when they ain't fucking around

Because Bears are big kids, they love to play games (and not all of them end up with having to reach for a cum towel). Many Bears are, or were, athletic at one point in their life (but Doritos have taken their toll). Conversely, they may have lived through the trauma of being picked last for gym class soccer. In either case, organized sports do not always draw Bears as participants. What does get them involved is the sense of team play as well as the uniforms. Who can resist oversized jerseys with big numbers on them, or coach shorts that make any butt look good? And of course there is the jockstrap, the accessory that works on the field and at the bar. The physical aspect of Bear sports is often thought of as helping to build a Bear's appetite (like it needs help). That means after the game Bears can have that extra beer or hot dog and not feel guilty about it.

Video Game Bears	
Real bears	*Bear Men*
Tekken III	*WWF Attitude*
Knock Out	*Mario*
Kings 99	*Myst - one of*
Crystal Castle	*the brothers*
Banjo Kazooie	*Ghost and*
	Goblins

Softball- Any progressive metropolitan area has an all-gay softball league. The Bear team is always the best team to watch and root for. If they lose, it is always in good spirit and usually to the all-lesbian team.

Bears in Sports

Rick Steiner/Wrestling

Craig Ironhead Heywood/St. Louis Rams

Louis Cyr/The Canadian Strong Man

Mike Ditka/Coach of Da Bears

Prince Albert/Wrestling

Craig "The Walrus" Stadler/PGA

Dan Fouts/San Diego Chargers

Dick Butkus/Announcer

Mike Holmgren/Seattle Seahawks Head Coach

Mark McGwire/St. Louis Cardinals
Single Season Home Run Record Holder

Wrestling- Not always as a participant but usually as a spectator, wrestling offers the closest thing to homoerotica allowed on TV. It comes in two forms: amateur and pro. Amateur wrestling has real-looking guys, usually from Eastern Bloc countries doing authentic Greco-Roman grappling on a mat. There is no glitz nor flying suplexes, but there is honest sweat on two men. Pro Wrestling is entirely different. The cocky wrestlers strut and flex about the ring in costumes that would do a drag queen proud. Often furry chests and bellies are exposed through shocking neon colored spandex and rhinestones.

Contact between competitors is not as intense as on the amateur level, but between the WCW, WWF and TNT Monday Nitro, the visual stimuli is good masturbatory fodder in case you didn't make it to the Adult Video store that night.

Football- Due to their size, Bears are often drafted to the football team in high school and may even play in college, but later in life he becomes, at best, an armchair quarterback. Superbowl Sunday holds a special place in many Bears' hearts because it's rugged beefy men, cool beer ads and a Broadway-style halftime show. It all boils down to Mike Ditka, and porn stories about locker rooms with communal showers.

Rugby- No helmets to hide the face, no shoulder pads to give the false impression of mass (or Joan Crawford), and thick legs make this British sport a favorite of Bears. Also, Rugby shirts are big, bulky and look good on any Bear.

Weightlifting- Typified by Alex Karras in the TV movie *The 500 Pound Jerk*, the Bear has a place in the Olympic Games, however some would debate whether or not lifting heavy objects is a sport. Even if it's not, the men in World's Strongest Man competitions, usually televised on ESPN2, are beefy and wear tight shorts.

Mah Jongg- The Bears' shared interest in this ancient game with Jewish matrons and Chinese women is baffling. The story that there was a secret society of Mah Jongg players at the Lone Star Saloon is Bear history. Bears would mysteriously disappear into the upstairs to a private club. What seemed like a wild sex party going on was merely big hairy guys sitting around throwing down tiles.

Winter Sports- The call of the ice is strong, but Bears make really strange looking figure skaters. The brutal sport of Hockey is more masculine, but murder on your mouth.

Professional Bears

Chicago Cubs	Orlando SolarBears
Chicago Bears	Salt Lake City Grizzlies
Boston Bruins	Vancouver Grizzlies
The Hershey Bears	North Sydney Bears

Go Bears!

a list of bear mascots

The bear as a college or Jr. college mascot occurs in 49 of the 50 states. Hawaii is the holdout. That means most guys can get to the college bookstore which will provide a plethora of tough bear tee shirts to fill a wardrobe.

The Bears

The basic college mascot: fight'n, proud and immortalized in a cheer by Jan Brady (Who's gonna win—THE BEARS—Say it again—THE BEARS). Thanks to Saturday Night Live these teams will always be referred to as Da Bears.

Athens State College	AL
Baylor University	TX
Bridgewater State College	MA
Brown University	RI
U of Central Arkansas	AR
Lenoir-Rhyne College	NC
Mercer University, Macon	GA
New York Institute of Technology	NY
NY State U at Potsdam	NY
U of Northern Colorado	CO
Pikeville College	KY
Rocky Mountain College	MT
Shaw University	NC
Shawnee State University	OH
Southern Christian University	FL
Southwest Missouri St. College	MO
U.S. Coast Guard Academy	CT
Ursinus College	PA
Washington University	MO

The Bruins

The Bruins- These colleges felt the need to be more than the black bear, which is what a bruin is, so they used the fancy shmancy name the Boston Hockey team uses.

Bellevue College	NE
Bethany College	CA
U of California, Los Angeles	CA
George Fox College	OR

The Grizzlies

Adams College	CO
Franklin College	IN
U of Montana	MT

The Bearcats- Ok, is it a Bear or is it a cat? Well, just grizzlies, but wanted to be associated with the Stutz.

Binghamton University	NY
Brescia College	KY
U of Cincinnati	OH
McKendree College	IL
Northwest Missouri St. Univ.	MO
Rust College	MS
St. Vincent's College	PA
Sam Houston State Univ.	TX
(but they're Bearkats with a K)	
Southwest Baptist University	MO
Willamette University	OR

The Polar Bears

or Nanooks if you've been named by Eskimos

U of Alaska	AK
Ohio Northern University	OH

The Golden Bears

The mascot of California

U of California, Berkley	CA
Kutztown University	PA
Miles College	AL
Morgan State College	MD
West Virginia Institute of Technology	WV
Western New England College	MA

Bears of Color

Livingston College	NC
home of the Blue Bears	
U of Maine	ME
home of the Black Bears	

The Great Outdoors
what a bear does in the woods, on a horse or on a coaster

Camping

This is not the camping that involves spouting *Valley of the Dolls* dialogue. It involves sleeping bags, pup tents and getting to shop at REI. This is the camping that makes man one with nature; Gives man the opportunity to breathe fresh air: This is the camping that the Boy Scouts never talk about. Camping ranges from the mobile home with air conditioning and indoor plumbing that hooks up at the gay campground to pulling a Brady Bunch and hiking down to the bottom of the Grand Canyon to sleep under the Arizona stars. In other words, when it comes to camping, you can go to either extreme, and Bears are apt for both. Roughing it has the most inherent sexuality and allure that attracts Bears. Making love al fresco with only the sounds of nature and a camp fire is the porn fantasy for anyone who ever watched a cowboy movie. Unfortunately, roughing it also has mosquitoes, the threat of rain and poorly cooked food because no one really knows how to cook on an open flame anymore. On the other hand, an RV vacation with all of its supposed amenities has its own drawbacks. Most RVs are not designed for larger men. Even the monster Winnebago is not conducive for two or three Bears to exist in harmony for any extended period of time. And Pop-up camper trailers just don't cut it when the couple on the one side gets frisky while the couple on the other side try to sleep.

Smokey the Bear was a real cub that survived a fire in the Capitan Mountains of New Mexico. He went on to become the symbol of forest fire prevention. In other words, he was the original Bear Fireman. There just hasn't been a beefcake calendar of him yet.

The Gay Rodeo Circuit

It takes a certain kind of Bear to tackle the rodeo and a pretty sturdy horse. But to the Bear men who always wanted to grow up and be a cowboy, this is their big chance. The Rodeo Circuit often conflicts with the Bear Event Weekend Circuit, so a choice must be made whether to ride a bucking bronco or ride a bucking Bear. Either way, by Monday morning you'll be walking a little funny.

Packing for the rodeo is totally different than packing for a Bear event. Hat boxes are needed for your Resistol Hats (and remember: Black felt before Easter and Straw after). Flannel shirts are replaced with Garth Brooks two-tone knockoffs and Cowbear butts are sqeezed into Wrangler's not the relaxed fit 501's.

However, be prepared. The Gay Rodeo attracts more than Bears. Faux Dollys, Patsys and Tammys, all with hair bigger than the Smoky Mountains, do the Watermelon Crawl and Doe-Se-Doe next to womyn that ride bulls as well as they can spit tobacco (they can do both better than most Bears).

Hot Fun in the Summertime

There is a faction of Bears who are obsessed with amusement parks. Many of them are members of A.C.E. (American Coaster Enthusiasts) an association that is willing to travel many a mile to eat bad BBQ served from a chow line and then  ride hideous body-tormenting roller coasters. Some of the torment is that coaster seats are not designed for wide butts, and shoulders that are good for football may not fit under a harness. Still Bears often find themselves strapped in, upside down with their legs in the air…on a looping steel coaster that is. For a wooden coaster, a Bear will travel to Kings Dominion in Virginia, to ride The Grizzly and buy the tee shirt. But Bears do not limit themselves to the Coasters. Dark Rides are always good for a grope and a Bear-filled log always makes the biggest splash at the flume ride. Water parks hold another special interest for Bears: Dads. Very often the Bearish men are found bobbing in the wave pool watching over a few rugrats. Hopefully he is the uncle and will take a little too long in the changing room! Bear events that are close to a Six Flags Park often have a day trip there.

Bear Hunting: Cruising for Sex

The blessing of being a Bear is that everybody loves a Bear: kids, senior citizens, women and men (thank goodness for the men). Bears are naturally friendly, also folks feel comfortable around them, so that translates to easy exchanges of conversation...
...and possibly phone numbers. The subtleties of communicating that you're a gay Bear, though, extends past saying the right words. There are clues a gay Bear relies on so that he does not have to come out and say he's gay; those who know the clues, get the Bear's story. Clues can be: 1. A Bear Built Tough tee shirt. It seems like it could be just another brand name of clothing like Eagle Outfitters or Big Dog. 2. Khaki shorts and construction boots. You won't find many straight Bears wearing this ensemble. 3. The discreet placement of the Bear Flag or paw print as a tattoo or watch face.

There have been times that even other gays don't realize that the Bear Flag is a derivative of the Rainbow Flag. The fact is that Bears are not obvious about their sexual orientation unless it's around each other. Bears are typically masculine and do not have the pretty boy looks that are stereotypically queer, so most Bears are perceived to be straight. Unlike straights, though, gay Bears crave hot, sweaty, man-on-man sex that could be the pay-off for cruising the right guy. Bear cruising is an art form unlike regular homo cruising, but not by much. There is still the glance across the bar that becomes a stare, the walk past him, the look back to see if he's looking, and the popular "if he follows me into the men's room then...." A Bear can and will usually start with an audible "woof" that is kin to a catcall. Flattery and the straightforward approach always works wonders.

Cruising on the Road

Rest areas on the highway have always been cruisy places, however vanity plates have made it easy to flirt while in motion. These plates can also double as your handle on AOL or IRC.

Bear pride shows

has a thing for TVLand

conceited youth

and a hairy butt

Shopping for Sex

The trick to Bear hunting is knowing where in the forest the Bear will be. Everyday places that have no intended sex appeal have a sexual energy that can be more powerful than a queer bar during a Black Out Party. It's kind of like the guy that doesn't know how cute he is. His naiveté makes him more desirable.

As Armistead Maupin chronicled in *Tales of the City* the supermarket is an optimal place for swinging singles. It stands to reason even more so for Bears: the place is stocked with food! Also check out good bakeries, not the Entenmann's outlet. Good bakeries have a take-a-number system that leaves girthy guys milling around eyeing one another's baked goods. Bears take pride in their dens, so home improvement and furnishing stores are high on this list. Places like hardware stores are a magnet for men, gay and straight, but it seems **Home Depot** has the market cornered on Bear men. They not only allow their

sales team to wear facial hair, but shorts too. Many a hairy calf can be seen on the forklift trying to get the spackle off the top shelf. The more common Bear populated areas of the store are the gardening, the lighting and the flooring departments. Home Depot also serves as a perfect middle ground for blind dates. The place is full of tests to see if the guy you just met on-line is worth a second date or

the classic

Carpe the Bear

looking for uncut

DMV won't allow

he makes noise in bed

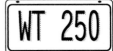

insert own dimension

just a hand job in the men's room. You can see if he knows how to handle a jigsaw, get his opinion on the new Ralph Lauren paint colors and find out if he even knows what caulk is. If he turns out not to be the right guy (even for the hand job) a trip to Home Depot is never wasted: Local contractors are often found in the lumber section for your viewing pleasure.

Bears are learned folk. Finding them in book and computer stores is a common experience. **Barnes and Noble** always has a good amount of fuzzy guys in the Art and Architecture, Gay and Lesbian, History or Magazine section. There are also comfy seats and a coffee bar, so the Bears will be relaxed enough to approach, however please remember that this is not the kind of bookstore with video booths in the back, so if you meet someone, take it outside. **CompUSA** also has a high frequency of Bear men. The love of current technology attracts the computer geek Bear like Trekkers to a Riker look-a-like contest. Cruising is most likely to take place in the hardware section where you both will be looking at the CUSeeMe package.

Unwritten Rules of Sex

When using food during sex, avoid Hershey's Kisses and rimming. It isn't pretty.

Goldschlager should never be used as a lubricant.

Kleenex + Cum = Glue

Leather is a rich man's sport.

Cum will hurt if it gets in your eye.

Bathhouse and Bookstore etiquette is as dictated as that behavior an Italian Mother would expect you to have in a Catholic Church.

probably a Bear

might be a Bear too

won't be a Bear

expect anything

and you can sit on it

will spend the night

Relationships for Bears

A Variation on Three-Ways

Friends

A Bear is always a good friend to have around. They have a good sense of humor and are great listeners. Their advice is often sought and well-heeded, because Bears seem to have the wisdom of an outsider that sees most things objectively. Very often Bears have many friends. Their AOL buddy list and address book is full of acquaintances and people they met only once. Bears are usually touchy/feely and would not think twice about going up to anybody and giving him or her a hug yet they never consider a sexual harassment lawsuit could follow. Because of their muscle and pick-ups, Bears are also important men to know when you move.

The Fuck Buddy

The special friend of a Bear is the Fuck Buddy. Bears have the ability to separate sex and love. When a Bear just wants to get off and not really have to deal with the emotions of a relationship or the cat-and-mouse games of a one night stand, he often calls on a friend who is also (and seemingly always) horny. Bears can fuck around and rumple the sheets and there are no strings attached. Fuck Buddies allow each Bear to experiment with new sex techniques that they just learned about on the web and laugh about it when one of them goes crashing onto the floor. The Fuck Buddy is not a one-Bear sort of relationship. Bears may have standing play dates with a few different men.

Couplehood

According to Leonard and Larry, "Domesticity isn't Pretty." When a Bear decides to marry that one man (and his friends will determine that he's married when he's been with this new guy for five dates) he will be loyal to that one man. That doesn't mean he won't fool around with someone else. Because of that "fuck buddy" mentality, Bears often have open relationships. *(see chart below)* Separating blowing some stranger to

The Open Relationship *(the darker the area the more frequent the sex)*

Monogamous
To the couple, there are no other bears. This stage occurs early and lasts a good month.

Cyber and Phone
Both partners are careful to only play with out of towners

the Happy Couple
In-town Bears
Out-of-town Bears

First Bear Event
Play with out of towners first. Locals are a last resort but not unheard of

the Happy Couple
In-town Bears
Out-of-town Bears

Post First Bear Event
Due to certain 'feelings,' both partners go back to monogamy

the Happy Couple
In-town Bears
Out-of-town Bears

get your own rocks off and caringly sucking off your significant other is easy to do if you're a Bear. One is down-and-dirty sex and the other one is love. Bear lovers will sometimes play together or sometimes play apart. Sometimes the other half will know, sometimes he'll be in the next room whipping up desserts for his lover and his lover's playmate. In any event, no matter where a Bear sticks his dick, his heart will always belong to that one man.

Phrases for Anal Sex

up the dirt road
travelin' the Hershey highway
drilling for oil
fishing for brown trout
fudge packing
buggering
corn-holin'

A Lesson in Rimming

Although rimming is a difficult technique to practice alone, there are exercises to work out the tongue muscle. This exercise is perfect for Bears because it involves sex and food. After putting a schmear of cream cheese on a split bagel, put the two halves together like a sandwich. Now, as the cream cheese seeps through the hole in the center, try eating the bagel from the center out. This will force you to use your tongue and take smaller bites, something Bears are not accustomed to. This exercise should not be done in the office on bagel day unless done for demonstration purposes.

Another technique that is also beneficial to both the receiver and the giver is the Alphabet Method. The rimmer should vary the movement by making letters with his tongue to avoid getting a cramp. This technique is also good for the rimmer who is only doing this to please his mate. It allows him to spell out nasty names for his lover or, if his mind wanders, a grocery list. However, beware: if the rimmie is very sensitive in the anal region, he may ask why you were spelling "Celery and Eggs."

When Opportunity Knocks	Safe Zone	Half & Half	Anything Goes
Both partners agree that sex can happen anytime anywhere with anyone- but it isn't looked for. One partner tends to have more opportunities	Sex with men either in or out of town that are Fuck Buddies and will pose no threat to the relationship. One partner will determine who is safe for the other	One partner plays- One partner doesn't. The one who doesn't is often nicknamed the Martyr. The one who does often keeps his proclivities a secret	Totally open and ready for action. These Bears play hard and work at it. Discussions of their sexual escapades are often a topic of conversation at the bar

A true "Fairy" tale - *The Three Bears*
a look at a three-way relationship

Once upon a time, there were three bears; a Papa Bear, a Mama Bear, and a Baby Bear. At least that's how the story we grew up with started. Now the three Bears mean something entirely different: it means a triangular relationship between three Bear men. More so in the Bear community than in the rest of the gay population, or even the straight population with the exception of Mormons, this makeshift family is an existence that is unique. The triad will usually start with a couple that adopts a cub (but it is not unheard of for a mama type Bear and cub to find a daddy). In either scenario the players take on the roles of those in the fairy tale. The Papa Bear is the oldest, and as tradition dictates, is usually the breadwinner. He will have a white-collar job or he will be an absentee dad enlisted in the military. He gives the impression of a top, but as with all Bears, the tougher they are, the higher the heels. The Mama Bear will arrange dinner parties and have a job that works out of the home (maybe real estate or interior decorating). He will be heavier than Papa Bear and perpetually joining and dropping out of Weight Watchers. He also has all the episodes of *Will and Grace* on tape. The Baby Bear will be a college student or a dropout that is being mentored by his two dads. He has the weakest of Beards but an incredible

mouth. It is possible that he stumbled into Papa and Mama's household to spice up their sex life, and if that is the case he will one day leave home. Together they are a family and they are also the social centerpiece of the local Bear club. Everyone wants to know how the *Three Bears* are doing.

The problems of this relationship would seem to be increased by a third over a more traditional one-on-one, however the opposite is true. As in any polygamous relationship that can be found in any cult in Arizona, all the participants know the pitfalls going into it, so level heads must prevail and the house is run like a democracy. Remember we are talking about three queers here. There will be back biting. There will be playing him against him, and like Family Circus, Ida Know and Not Me will make an appearance ("Who didn't put the cap on the lube?" "not me," "I don't know"). But like a family, the benefits are also there. The increased love, the family dinners and the combinations of who screws who. As in the story, they will have an open door policy at their house welcoming any traveler that finds them, usually via the Internet web site Baby Bear has designed. Unlike the fairy tale, there are not three beds but one California King. And they all sleep in it.

RED ALERT

Beware of those who seem like Bears

Most gay Bears can spot another gay Bear, but you might accidentally cruise one of these guys. He may be cute. He may be smiling at you. And he may have a beard. But he does not want to go to bed with you because he's straight and may be narrow. Look for the signs and recognize these pseudo Bears:

POW-MIA Looks like a Bear and loves his fellow fighting soldier, but does not want to dig in your foxhole. *Warning signs-* Stars and Stripes bandana around his head. Fatigue jacket. A "Don't Blame Me, I voted for Bush" bumper sticker.

Biker Looks like a Bear, acts like a Bear, may even think your come-ons are cute but he's looking for tits and ass without hair on them. *Warning signs-* the leather he's wearing looks like it's been worn more than just on Saturday nights at the Hellfire Club. Biker Babe close behind, who will "kill you if you don't stop lookin' at her man." The sticker on his helmet says Christian Biker Association.

Amish Looks like a Bear (his beard is usually full but there's no mustache) and he even dresses in black, but unless you brought your Bible, forget it. He'll tolerate you, but you won't raise his barn. *Warning signs-* a buggy.

The Opposite Sex

It's more than a musical starring June Allyson

Women Bears Love
Mom
Sara Lee
Mrs. Butterworth
Betty Crocker
Aunt Jemima

Bisexual Bears

In comparison to the rest of the gay community, there are more than a ton of bisexual Bears. These men have had or are still having, sex with women while also playing around with big hairy men. These Bears fall into one of three categories:

The Swinger. His wife knows and plays too. This is the most interesting Bear because she entered the marriage knowing her husband's tastes. She also likes Bears and usually women too. Their life together is an endless orgy. He is rare, but not unheard of.

The Closet Case. His wife doesn't know or at least he thinks she doesn't. The married Bear cruises bookstores, IRC and restrooms. He is most likely a professional. This Bear often graduates to the born-again Bear.

The Born-Again Bear. He has been re-born as a homosexual after a divorce. He is very common and usually older. He will have a voracious sexual appetite and grandchildren.

Goldilocks The Bear Fag Hag

Few women enter the cave of the Bear bar. Even the standard, slightly chubby (usually rhinestone studded) Fag Hag rarely enters. Bear bars are men's bars, and the clientele does not overtly seem like the jovial queens a Hag is drawn to. The few women that do enter into the cave, however, find that Bears are far from the mean beasts that feast on little girls lost in the woods. And not only aren't those Bears scary, but the girls ain't so innocent. The women that do make it there have a certain toughness that likens them to biker chicks. She is no lady, she's a broad. She wears a leather vest, has pierced nipples, spiked hair and an ear cuff. She is most likely a lesbian who is unattached. Her function is unclear: she does not play the mother role to Bears because most Bears cook better than she does. She is not a Bear's confidant, as most Bears rely on their bartender. Bears look at her as their equal. Sexually, she may be drawn to Bears (she enjoys a good Bear fuck video) and Bears find her charming. She may be the one woman they would sleep with for experimental reasons. But for the most part, she will be the mascot to the local Bear club.

Women Who Could Be Bears
Rosie O'Donnell
Camryn Manheim
Roseanne
Delta Burke
Hattie McDaniel
Margaret Cho
Oprah
Edie McClurg
Dolly Parton
Lea DeLaria
Special Case:
  Liz Taylor.
  When weight
  was an issue.

Compare and Contrast
Bear to LesBruin, the female of the species

There is a faction in the lesbian community of female types that exude an incredible amount of the same qualities as the Bear man. They have been called Bull Dykes, Diesel Dykes, just Dykes or Janet Reno, however a more appropriate name for them is LesBruins. Just as Bears represent only a minority in the male gay community, Lesbruins are also a select few. To compare and contrast the Bear and the Lesbruin is like comparing bananas to melons: sure they're different but they are still both fruits:

Both will wear flannel shirts, but his will come from Eddie Bauer.
Both will have sex toys, but hers will be industrial.
Both will wear COACH brand shorts, but he'll complain they make his ass look big.
Both will shop at AutoZone, but she will not need help from a salesman.

Both will have good music collections, but she will have all the Indigo Girls CDs, he'll only have a few.
Both will rent Bear videos, but he will have blown at least one of the actors.
Both will have a crush on their high school gym teacher, but hers will be consummated.
Both will drive pickups, but his will be an automatic.
Both will get the same haircut at the same barber, but hers will cost more.
Both will have dry cleaning .....well maybe she won't.
Both will wear work boots, but she will wear them to a wedding.
Both will enjoy golf, but he has windmills on his course.
Both will like Jodie Foster, but she will like her more. A whole lot more.
Both will own cats, but hers will definitely be a male and castrated.
Both will have weight problems, and while he drinks Slim-Fast, she'll eat Jenny Craig.

Bear Quiz 4 - Jack's Great Card Hunt

Jason

e-mail
jrobbie@ aol.com

1

Joey Cosloski
706-555-3993
B4fw+ke++

2

Jimmy Rudinski
407-555-7463

3

Jr. Peterson
PO BOX 929
Nashville Tenn.
615-555-MEAT

4

BtmBear(irc)

Just Say **WOOF!**

houston tx

5

BIG CITY BANK
J R Polk
Branch Manager

JRPeter@bcbank.com
4111 Peachtree Street Atlanta Ga 19032
404-555-3000 fax 404-555-3010

6

---

the Dilemma Jack went to Southern Decadence and had safe sex with 6 men (It was a slow year). On the last day he met up with the guy who fucked him the best, only he couldn't remember his name, nor any of the names of any of his partners. The guy gave Jack a trick card and he slipped it into his pocket along with the other trick cards he had collected, without looking at it. Using the information Jack gathered from his meeting can you help Jack determine who the best fucker was?

the Conversation: He mentioned a lover who couldn't make the trip, he drove to NOLA and it took him about 10 hours. He worked in computers but bartended at night. He still receives the BML but canceled his AOL account at Christmas when he got his new PC. A buddy of his came up and called him JR, but he didn't seem to like it. Jack recalled from the night before somone on the street called him something Polish sounding. He had a great beard and a fuzzy ass.

the Solution: It really got down to who it wasn't. Any one of them could have been a JR but No.4 didn't look like him, No.1 was still on AOL and a self respecting Bear would update his cards prior to an event. The guy was a top so that ruled out No.5 and No.6 gave him a business card that was the wrong business and tacky. That left No.2 or 3. He called Jimmy in Orlando, about 10 hours away but it was disconnected. So he called Joey, the right Bear Code indicated his looks were right, in LaGrange Ga. also about 10 hours away. Joey and Jimmy had a commitment ceremony the following summer. Joey's father, Joe Sr., gave his son away.

CHAPTER FIVE
THE LEFTOVERS

what doesn't fit anywhere else
or
"Oh! There's leftovers? Yummy!"

Fur-nacular

It is possible that a Bear doesn't realize he is a Bear. Once he discovers this community however, it could take a good period of time before he can master the gist of Beardom. Learning the politics of the Bear community is a laborious and an ongoing process. Even those Bears who have a copy of Bear Magazine Issue 1 still find out new things about the community with every event they attend. To help make the communication easier among Bears, this lexicon has been provided so that they may interact verbally as well as physically.

Admirer *n.* one who has a thing for Bears but isn't necessarily one

Arkansas luggage *n.* foreskin

Baloo *name.* Mowgli's fun-loving mentor in Kipling's *The Jungle Book*

Bart the Bear *name.* The real live bear that graced the cover of LIFE and has starred in many movies

Bear *n.* a big hairy bearded homosexual man. If you didn't get it by this point in the book, re-read chapter 1

Bearish *adj.* To have the physical qualities of a Bear

bear claw *n.* A tasty pastry in the shape of the ursine appendage

Bear God *n.* the perfect Bear, but too perfect to be approachable at the bar. He will go home alone most nights

bear in mind *Colloq.* To have a mental picture of a specific Bear in your mind's eye while masturbating

Bear meat *n.* a Bear's cock

bare naked *adj.* To be disrobed and without shame

bear necessities *n.* the simple things in life that can be bought with an American Express card

Abbreviations

A.T.N.A	All Talk No Action— a dick tease
B.O.B.	Big 'Ol Bottom
B.D.U.	Battle Dress Uniform. This is used by those into military drag
B.M.L.	Bears Mailing List
I.M.L.	International Mr. Leather
I.L.M.	Industrial Light and Magic. The place where sci-fi movies come from
I.R.C.	Internet Relay Chat
I.B.C.	Rootbeer served at the bar to recovering alcoholics
I.B.R.	International Bear Rendezvous
T.M.I	Too Much Information
W.T.M.I	Way Too Much Information
W.L.T.-T.L.J	Walks Like Tarzan — Talks Like Jane
W.W.F.	World Wrestling Federation
W.C.W.	World Championship Wrestling
G.S.T.	Gay Standard Time — approx.35 minutes late
C.B.T.	Cock and Ball Torture
T.T.	Tit Torture
T.T.F.N.	Ta Ta For Now — ala Tigger
S.&M.	Sadism and Masochism
M&M	Tasty Bite-sized Candy

The Lone Star Handshake

Not necessarily a secret handshake in the traditional Kiwanis sorta way, but a more universal way of knowing that the man whose hand you're shaking has been around.

How is it done?
The key to the Lone Star Shake is not in the hand placement or motion, but in the eyes, neck and head. As you begin a standard handshake and while exchanging pleasant greetings, move your head side-to-side avoiding all eye contact with your partner. He will most likely be doing the same. The reason behind this motion is to scope out the room, looking to see if there is anyone better that you should be cruising.

Beary Poppins *n.* A Bear that has all the morals of Julie Andrews. *"It takes more than a spoonful of sugar to make that Beary Poppins go down."*

Bear scrum *n.* three or more Bears in a huddle, arm and arm with at least one dick exposed

Bearaphernalia *n.* Bear stuff. *"Once I explained to my family what a Bear is, every year, for my birthday I get teddy bears and all that other Bearaphernalia crap."*

Bearister *n.* a Bear lawyer

Berenstain Bears *name.* a family of bears with curiously long snouts created by Jan and Stan Berenstain

behr *n.* a Bear that is not bearded but moustached, usually for work reasons

-berg *suffix.* mountain home of the Bear People

Big Al *name.* The audioanimatronic Bear in the Country Bear Jamboree at the Magic Kingdom. Available in plush

big pants *n.* To have a hard-on ala Suzanne Sugarbaker. "He's got the big pants for Al Roker"

blue collar *adj.* That which is associated with power-tools

BooBoo *name.* Yogi's "little friend"

bottom *n.* 1. The position one takes when pursuing a straight man. 2. The position one takes when in bed with a top. 3. The one who won the coin toss. *v.* to be in the submissive and vulnerable position and still be pushy.

bruin *n.* just another word for Bear

bubba *n.* a good ol' boy from the south with a pick-up

bubble butt *n.* a fleshy derriere with a distinctive shape. *See Sir Mix-A-Lot*

butch *adj.* he who can change his own spark plugs

Captain Kangaroo *name.* Kiddie show host who is now played by a man with a chin curtain

Captain Kangaroo's Dancing Bear *name.* A man in a bear costume portraying a politically incorrect animal abuse scenario

cave *n.* a Bear's bedroom

chaser *n.* see admirer, but apply to chubbies

chubby *n.* 1. a member of Girth and Mirth, a Bear with little to no body or facial hair, or someone who does not kowtow to Jenny Craig. 2. **chubby, chub-on.** A hard on. *"Al Roker gave him a chubby."*

chubby chaser *n.* see chaser

circuit bear *n.* he who works the room at a Bear event

credit queen *n.* the Bear who has to stay at the end of the movie because he knows someone on the special effects team or one of the animators

cybear *n.* a Bear attached to his keyboard and the Internet

cyber *n.* the type of sex you deny having over the web at 3am

Daddy Bear *n.* He who is closer to Christmas in the May/December romance. Gray hair is required.

dancing Bear *n.* once a twink who still thinks he is Tony Manero or Marge Champion

deadhead Bears *n.* the scraggly Bears who emulate Jerry Garcia

den *n.* the Bear habitat that is tastefully decorated

dick tease *n.* he kisses, he touches, he gropes but he will not put out

dinner *n.* euphemism for sex when talking to your partner about a fuck buddy. *"I went over to Jake's house for dinner while you were working."*

drag *n.* any themed clothing, e.g., biker drag, military drag or Bear business drag

---

Vo-Cub-ulary
words for the Gen-X Bears

bearly legal *adj.* old enough to go to a Bear event but not old enough to appreciate it.

cub *n.* 1 a young Bear, 2 a smaller bear, 3 a baseball player from Chicago

cub cake *n.* a pastry in which the filling is desirable

cubby hole *n.* place where pastry filling is injected. *name.* Bar in Fort Lauderdale

cubholio *slang.* variation from Beavis and Butthead Cornholio

house cub *n.* 1 the young man servant, 2 the third in a relationship, 3 the young Bear who is a DJ

huscub *n.* the married cub

my cub runneth over *Colloq.* notes a cub that has imbibed too much or has been on his back too much

talk to the paw *Colloq.* from Springer or Lake. Said with arm extended and hand in a vertical position

woofever *slang.* indifference, the lacksadaisical comeback associated with "whatever."

Ewok *name.* Tribe of primitive teddy bears with teeth that inhabit Endor

exu-bear-ant *adj.* full of gusto, initiator of sex

Fem *adj.* he who has the traits of she

fembot *n.* a twink or "Castro" clone

Fozzie Bear *name.* the bear muppet. *n.* a goofball that is loud at parties

frottage *verb.* rubbing against a partner's body. Also known as the Princeton Rub.

fur *n.* body hair

furball *n.* term of endearment for one who is hairy to a fault

furry *adj.* excessive body hair

fuzz *n.* 1. fur lite 2. beginnings of a beard

Gender fuck *n.* a once-a-year drag queen with a beard who refuses to shave

Gentle Ben *name.* the real bear from the 60's television show of the same name.

glory hole *n.* an opening in a partition or wall, large enough to accommodate the male genitals for the purpose of stimulation on the other side. *See Greyhound Terminal or Sears*

glazed doughnut *n.* he who is coated with the semen of one or more Bears

going commando *adj.* to go without underwear

grizzly *adj.* from the French grizel meaning somewhat grey or grayish

Grizzly Adams *name.* a better heart-throb than Bobby Sherman

grisly *n.* from the Anglo-Saxon grislic, meaning horrible

grizm *n.* the Bear version of semen

grrrrr *interjection.* Sound made by a Bear when satisfied, hungry or in heat

growl *exclamation.* Word used to express desire or annoyance

gummi *n.* from German. 1 the substance used in making rubber clothing, not suitable for those with fur. 2 secret ingredient in Gummi Bears

Gummi Bears *name.* tasty little rubbery snacks imported from Germany

---

How to say "bear" in sign language:

Hair Bear Bunch *name.* The 70's Hanna-Barbera cartoon of three wild bears in a zoo. Paul Lynde voiced the Zoo Keeper.

hammam *n.* a Turkish bath house

has-Bear *n.* a Bear that has been around the block too many times. Most of the Bear community has seen him naked.

Hedda Hopbear *n.* He who has all the hottest gossip at the bar. "If you want the dirt on why you-know-who doesn't come around anymore, ask Hedda Hopbear."

hi-bear-nation *v.* the act of cuddling together or snuggling *n.* Bear event held by the Show Me Bears

Hill Billy Bears *name.* Family of Ozark bears featured on the Banana Splits show

hirsute *n.* a full pelt of body hair

Humphrey *name.* Disney animated bear that lives in the National Parks and in film shorts with The Ranger, J. Audubon Woodlore

husbear *n.* your significant other

Jacruizzi *n.* a hot tub that sees lots of action *"The water in the jacruizzi was clear before Bear Bust."*

Jesse Dukes *n.* the male version of Daisy Dukes, cut-off jeans that are cut way too short. May be illegal in some states

Libearian *n.* 1 a Bear that works in the library or bookstore 2 a Bear that works the "bookstores"

Lucky Pierre *n.* member of a three-way who ends up in the middle

Mangina *n.* 1 the crevice on a male in which another male stimulates

The Lucky Shirt

You can't remember where you got it, but you like to wear it. You look good in it, it fits and you have always gotten laid whenever you wear it. It is your lucky shirt and every stain on it has been earned. This shirt could have been in a previous chapter because it is an article of clothing or used for cruising, but because it collects a souvenir of every Bear run you go to, it belongs with the other leftovers. This lucky charm or talisman does not necessarily need to be a shirt. Some Bears have lucky shorts, sure-fire boots, or a never fail jockstrap.

pie
Fiesta de los
Osos '99

duck sauce
IBR
Dim sum '95

bbq sauce
TBRU '98

sweat
Southern
Decadence '97

Carlos
Bear Invasion '96

dirt
Hillside Campground '99

mustard from a
Chicago hotdog
Bear Pride '94

Anthropomorphin

Many people will associate Bears with a culture of people who live in a fantasy world of animal people. They are either the Nastassia Kinski type from *Cat People* that turn into a real animal or the Ron Perlman type from TV's *Beauty and the Beast*, the kind that are half human, half animal. They call themselves **Yiffies** and although there are some Ren or Scifi Bears that subscribe to the talisman and folklore of their inner grizzly, most Bear men prefer sex with a man that acts like an animal in bed and isn't going to morph into one.

his penis. 2 a man's anus when used in a sexual manner. *"He created his mangina by crossing his legs and letting me fuck between his thighs."*

muscle Bears *n.* bears who have spent time at Gold's Gym and usually a lot of mirrors. Obsessed with pro wrestling

Papa Bear *n.* an older Bear with white hair and beard. Has an increased sex drive

parachute *n.* sexual device attached to the scrotum with weights for the purpose of stretching

playtime *n.* a period in a date, or instead of a date, when sex is being had

playdate *n.* a set date and time for sex and nothing more

Pooh, Winnie the *name.* silly willy nilly old bear stuffed with fluff

Raunch *n.* hardcore sex involving bodily functions and/or apparati that can be purchased at automotive stores or Lechter's. Will involve clean up.

redneck *n.* a bubba with an attitude, a gun rack in the car and a passion for Jeff Foxworthy

rimming *v. "It's when you put you legs behind your head and someone licks your ass."* Mrs. Cartman, Eric's Mom

Ruth Anne *n.* a rest area on a highway that cruises

Sasquatch *n.* 1 Bigfoot, 2 the creature that terrifies the northwest, 3 the guy at the pool who looks like he has on a sweater

scat *n.* shit

significant otter *n.* the half of a relationship who is just shy of being a Bear. See Related Animals

Sitges *n.* gay town in Northeast Spain, close to Barcelona

Related Animals

The Otter - a skinny hairy guy who hangs around with Bears. Big into the local Bear club.

The Wolf - an aging otter that has retained his good looks. Not a Troll.

The Gym Peacock - usually hairless and buff. Wears the skimpiest of clothes.

The Disco Bunny - too coifed and energetic to hang around with the Bears, but they sometimes find the way to that part of the forest. They make good sidekicks and are entertaining, if nothing else.

abridged
The ^V Hanky Code

More of a leather thing than a Bear thing, this silent way for gay men to communicate has been around for decades now. Although its popularity has diminished, it is still common to see a Bear man "flagging red right" at the Lone Star. By placing a certain color bandana in one's back pocket, he tells the gay world how he likes it and with whom. It is a system that could only work with gay men, for it takes a special type of male to differentiate between robin's egg and light blue in a dimly lit bar.

For the most part, the left side equals Dominant and the right side equals Submissive. This same placement works for nipple rings and keys on chains.

worn on left	color	worn on right
sm top	black	sm bottom
bondage	grey	tie me up
wants head	lt blue	gives head
69er	robin's egg	all but 69
cop	med blue	copsucker
fucker	navy blue	fuckee
cbt	teal blue	cbt bottom
fister	red	fistee
cuts	maroon	bleeds
pisser	yellow	pissee
hung 8"	mustard	wants 8"+
2 for 1	gold	1 for 2
hustler	kelly green	john
daddy	hunter	orphan boy
military	olive drab	military
rimmer	beige	rimmee
scat top	brown	scat bottom

slurp *interj.* 1 Noise made by Bears while having sex. 2 popular on-line greeting

slut *n.* the Bear that does it, does it a lot, and is proud of it

Smokey the Bear *name.* Spokesbear for the Nation's parks promoting forest fire prevention

spinner *n.* a cub or otter small enough to twirl in bed

star fucker *n.* he who dates or plays with only those who have attained status in the Bear community

Steiff *name.* Company in Germany responsible for expensive and hard teddy bears

stroller daddy *n.* good looking men at theme parks or malls pushing a baby carriage. They will most times cruise you first

Teddy bear *n.* 1 a smaller-than-life stuffed toy that is intentionally designed to evoke emotions of love and caring. 2 a larger-than-life man who has designed himself to evoke emotions of lust

Teddy Ruxpin *n.* a talking teddy bear that has a solid plastic center making it difficult to cuddle

The Country Bear Jamboree *name.* The attraction at the Magic Kingdom of Disney that has folks hoopin' and hollerin' with audioanimatronic bears. Popular on Gay Day.

top *n.* 1 The other position one takes when pursuing a straight man. 2 The position one takes when in bed with a bottom. 3 The one who lost the coin toss. *v.* to be in the dominant position and still be told what to do

trapper *n.* the man that caught himself a Bear for purposes of marriage. Usually a twink or otter. *See Admirer*

trucker *n.* fantasy sex partner who drives at least an 18 wheeler and you met him in a Ruth Anne

twink *n.* the cliché: smaller, effeminate, nelly homosexual man

Unbearable *adj.* a Bear that is less than tolerated on-line, at bear events or the bar

uncle(s) *n.* the two men seen with a child or children. The pair deems that one of them at least is not the biological parent, and is therefore the lover of the other and suitable for cruising

ursine *n.* Bear-like

ursus *n.* the Latin for bear

Versatile *n.* 1 someone afraid to say they are a bottom. 2 to play either the top or bottom role during sex

Watersports *n.* sex acts involving urine

wife beater *n.* a ribbed tank top undershirt that shows the most hair on the chest, back and shoulders

woody *n.* a hard-on

woofer *n.* term of endearment from one Bear to another

Wookie *n.* species of large hairy beasts made popular by Chewbacca

wrestle *v.* the supposed non-sexual version of male to male intimacy sanctioned by the International Olympic Committee

Yogi *name.* The popular cartoon bear with a thing for picnic baskets and Boo Boo

Your cave or mine? *Colloq.* Pick-up line that never works

The word is WOOF!

The origin of the term "woof" and its introduction into the Bear vocabulary is cloudy. It has been debated ad nauseam on the BML and no one has come up with a definitive answer. The fact of the matter is that "woof" is the primary mode of communication between Bears. What does it mean? It is usually meant as "I think you are one hot, sexy Bear whom I'd like to rub fur with." "Woof" is just easier to say. It can also be interpreted as a form of approval. For instance, a Bear is saying on AOL that he's into kissing, cuddling, 69ing and getting plowed. The Bear he is talking to would respond "woof!" meaning he's into that as well. It can also be interpreted as a form of "hello" and "good-bye," making it the Bear equivalent of Aloha or Shalom. Finally, it is the universal secret word used by Bears. It is put on tee shirts and baseball caps to identify the wearer as a team player. It is used also as a discreet way of determining if your gaydar was correct about the Bear you're passing in the street. Saying "woof" just loud enough that he can hear will make him do one of two things: pass and not know what you're saying or "woof" back at you. This will be your confirmation.

Final Bear Quiz- Are You A Bear?

On a separate piece of paper, track your score. Answer each question honestly and to the best of your knowledge

Part 1
Start with your weight
+ your age
+ 100 pts for being gay
+ 50 pts for being bi
+ 30 pts for being straight

Part 2 Physical
+ the % of body hair (Remember, except for those Mexican kids in the circus, no one is 100%)
- 50 pts for every inch your hair is above your head
+ 50 pts for a full beard
+ 40 pts for a goatee
+ 30 pts for a mustache
+ 20 pts for unshaven
- 10 pts for a mole with a hair on your chin
+ 5 pts for black hair
+ 5 pts for blonde hair
+ 5 pts for red hair
+ 5 pts for brown hair
+ 5 pts for gray hair
+ 5 pts for no hair
- 20 pts for any highlights or dye jobs
+ the size of your jeans
- the size you should be wearing
+ 20 pts if you have a gym membership
+ 30 pts if you dropped out
+ 5 pts for each flannel shirt
+ 10 pts if the sleeves are ripped out
- 20 pts if it's a size S or M
+ 20 pts for every X over XL

+ 10 pts for cutting your own hair
+ 30 pts if you go to a barbershop
- 15 pts if you go to a salon

Part 3 At Home
+ 20 pts for a computer
+ 30 pts if it's a MAC
+ 10 pts for each power tool
+ 40 pts for a glue gun, sewing machine or Kitchen Aid
+ 40 pts for each TV and VCR
- 10 pts if it's Beta
+ 5 pts for each Barbra and Bette Midler CD
+ 10 pts for each Broadway Cast CD
+ 30 pts for each Country/ Western CD
+ 10 pts for any automobile nicknamed "The Boat"
+ 15 pts for a sport utility vehicle
+ 20 pts for a truck
+ 50 pts for a Semi
- 30 pts for a Miata
+ 40 pts for vanity plates alluding to Bears

Part 4 Social
+ 1 point for every Bear bar you've been to
+ 6 pts if you went home with someone
+ 50 pts for each organized Bear event you've attended
+ the mileage to the event or the cost of your airline ticket, whichever is more
- 300 pts if you didn't have sex
+ 5 pts for every Bear you have on your AOL Buddy List

+ 10 pts for each buddy you've met
+ 15 pts if you fucked 'em
+ 15 pts for each colored hanky you own
+ 20 pts if it's been used to cruise with
+ 30 pts if it was used successfully
+ 69 pts if the words 'glory hole' mean anything to you
+ 7 pts per bartender that knows you by name or what you drink
+ 2 pts for every issue of Bear or American Bear you own
+ 10 pts for every model you've been with
+ 100 pts if you posed
+ 3 pts for every teddy bear you own

Scoring

If you have any score at all, you are not a Bear, because a real Bear wouldn't give a hoot about how well he scored. He knows he's a Bear because he KNOWS he a Bear. Simply put, any man who thinks he's a Bear is a Bear.

Now that you've read it, click it!
click it!
www.bearhandbook.com
where you can voice your feedback
(please note web site rule on page 66)

Order Your Own Copy of
This Important Book for Your Personal Library!

THE BEAR HANDBOOK
A Comprehensive Guide for Those Who Are Husky, Hairy, and Homosexual and Those Who Love 'Em

_____in hardbound at $39.95 (ISBN: 1-56023-996-4)

_____in softbound at $14.95 (ISBN: 1-56023-997-2)

COST OF BOOKS_____

OUTSIDE USA/CANADA/
MEXICO: ADD 20%_____

POSTAGE & HANDLING_____
(US: $3.00 for first book & $1.25
for each additional book)
Outside US: $4.75 for first book
& 1.75 for each additional book)

SUBTOTAL_____

STATE TAX_____
(NY, OH & MN residents, please
add appropriate local sales tax)

FINAL TOTAL_____
(If paying in Canadian funds,
convert using the current
exchange rate. UNESCO
coupons welcome.)

☐ **BILL ME LATER:** ($5 service charge will
be added) (Bill-me option is good on
US/Canada/Mexico orders only: not good
to jobbers, wholesalers, or subscription
agencies.)

☐ Check here if billing address is
different from shipping address and
attach purchase order and billing
address information.

Signature _____

☐ **Payment Enclosed: $**_____
☐ **Please Charge to My Credit Card.**

☐Visa ☐ MasterCard ☐ AmEx
☐ Discover ☐ Diners Club

Account # _____

Exp. Date _____

Signature _____

Prices in US dollars and subject to change without notice

NAME _____

INSTITUTION _____

ADDRESS _____

CITY _____

STATE/ZIP _____

COUNTRY _____COUNTY (NY residents only) _____

TEL _____FAX _____

E-MAIL _____
May we use your e-mail address for confirmations and other types of information? ☐ Yes ☐ No

Order From Your Local Bookstore or Directly From
The Haworth Press, Inc.
10 Alice Street, Binghamton, New York 13904-1580 ● USA
TELEPHONE: 1-800-HAWORTH (1-800-429-6784) / Outside US/Canada: (607) 722-5857
FAX: 1-800-895-0582 / Outside US/Canada: (607) 772-6362
E-mail: getinfo@haworthpressinc.com
PLEASE PHOTOCOPY THIS FORM FOR YOUR PERSONAL USE.

BOF96